Dr. Jane Carswell

Family Physician

Humanitarian

Friend

Dr. Jane Carswell

Family Physician, Humanitarian, Friend

Gretchen Griffith

GRETCHEN GRIFFITH

With

KENNETH ROBERTS

Non-Fiction/Biography
Cover designs – Books that Matter
Front cover photo – Spencer Ainsley, Lenoir *News-Topic,*
photo restored and colorized by Bill Tate
Cover roses – Jane Carswell, back photo restored by Douglas Terry
Unless otherwise credited, interior photographs were taken by the author
or are from the personal collection of Kenneth Roberts and Jane Carswell.

Gretchen Griffith, Publisher, Lenoir, North Carolina
Printed in Columbia, South Carolina
Library of Congress Control Number: 2018905127
ISBN-13:978-1717108685
ISBN-10:1717108687

Dedicated To

Jane Triplett Carswell
For all the love she brought

TABLE OF CONTENTS

Preface

When Ken Roberts approached me about writing a biography of his late wife, Dr. Jane Carswell, my first question was, "Would she be okay with this?"

"Probably not," he replied. "But it's too important not to share."

He was right. From all my discussions with her friends and colleagues, she was an extremely private person who preferred the spotlight to focus on others while she worked behind the scenes. She was the first to give others the credit, and yet her own story is too remarkable not to bring out into the open as an inspiration. She thought out solutions to society's limitations. She stepped up when she saw a need and she lived her faith as she practiced her medicine.

Much of this book was written by Jane herself. Not only was she a hard working physician, a dedicated humanitarian and a friend to many, she was a prolific writer who set her thinking in words that have lived well beyond her life. She was also an accomplished photographer. Included at the beginning of each chapter are pictures showcasing Jane's gift in nature photography.

As I wrote, I kept in mind her unpretentiousness, the choices she made to remain in the background, and the angst it might have caused her knowing I was laying bare the details of her life. I had to weigh that against the fullness of her narrative and what being Dr. Jane Carswell actually meant. In the end, the need to show the reader the complete story overshadowed any hesitancy I might have had. I thank Ken Roberts for entrusting me with this story, for it was Jane's to tell. I merely allowed her legacy to speak for her.

Gretchen Griffith

Foreword

When Jane Carswell arrived in Lenoir, North Carolina in 1961 to practice medicine, she was twenty-nine years old, single, five foot two, and weighed a mere hundred ten pounds. She knew no one in town before signing a contract with Dr. Vernon Blackwelder to serve at his hospital, and no one in her family lived closer than a five hour drive. In a short time, Jane went from being a "stranger" to becoming one of the best known and most loved citizens in the county.

With the difficulties women experienced in being accepted into medical schools in the first half of the twentieth century, it is incredible that three outstanding women physicians practiced in the small town of Lenoir at the same time during the sixties, Dr. Caroline McNairy, Dr. Marjorie Strawn, and Jane. People often asked her how hard it was as a woman to establish a medical practice here in Lenoir. Her answer was always, "It was easy because Dr. McNairy and Dr. Strawn paved the way."

Dr. Charles Scheil came to Lenoir in 1964. He and Jane soon established a practice together. Both were highly qualified, so their practice prospered. I was Dr. Scheil's patient until he retired. Jane became good friends with Charlie and his wife, Fran, and later it was my privilege to join that friendship group.

Although her medical practice was her initial path to meeting people, she reached out in other ways. She joined the First Presbyterian Church of Lenoir, a perfect fit for her, where she found a congregation anxious to serve the needs of the community. Like most denominations in those years, the Presbyterian Church did not allow women to serve as officers. When that rule was relaxed, Jane became the first woman ruling elder of the First Presbyterian Church of Lenoir.

Jane played as hard as she worked. She immediately joined a bowling league, played tennis, hiked and backpacked in the mountains, went cross country skiing in winter, and took up nature photography. She was an exceptional traveler who soaked in everything she saw.

High on the list of what was important to Jane were the nearby Blue Ridge Mountains, a place of solitude for her, yet a place for many of her favorite activities with friends.

Author Gretchen Griffith tells the fascinating story of Jane's life from birth to her sudden and way too soon death. She will tell you how Jane and I met and married two years later to become two of the happiest people in the world as we enjoyed an active retirement and grandchildren who enriched both our lives.

Who should read this book? Young people who are preparing for challenging careers, especially nontraditional ones for their gender; People of faith searching for inspiration; People who want to read a good, heartwarming success story; And finally, her many friends who want to know more about her life since she talked very little about herself. This book speaks for her.

Ken Roberts

Part I

FAMILY
PHYSICIAN

1

Heritage

**"The best thing parents can give
is a Christian Heritage and a good education."**
Jane Carswell in the *Sandhills Citizen*
December 12, 1984

Dr. Jane Triplett Carswell was in the midst of a stellar career when she guest lectured at the Medical College of Virginia where she had completed her schooling and residency. Still in the limelight from being selected as the 1984-85 national Family Physician of the Year, she spoke to the students sitting where she once sat. They were destined to become practitioners of a unique brand, Family Physicians, and she was giving them words of wisdom from the trenches.

Doctors often enter into their careers with "delusions of grandeur," she began, but added, "The cure is a few weeks of practicing medicine." She went on to advise them that the key to successful family practice is "community involvement with a good dose of humility." She encouraged them to go beyond treating symptoms to search for the underlying cause of the problem, to study who people were, and to look at their feelings, hopes, schedules, and relationships. "Caring for the patient is caring about the patient," she said. (*Family Practice Hi-Lights*, Medical College of Virginia Student Family Practice Association, Winter, 1984)

She neglected to disclose a few details of what made her a beloved physician, especially with the elderly widows who dressed in their Sunday best for a doctor visit to her and were gifted with a fresh rose Jane had snipped in her yard that morning on her way to work. Nor did she mention attending weddings of patients, nor the many school programs and graduations. No, these physicians would uncover their own uniqueness in their time, just as she had. She did talk about the years she listened to her patients share about their jobs, their religions, their politics, and their hopes and fears, anything that would help her understand the person sitting before her. She realized full well interactions within families had an impact on her patients' health.

She was guarded, however, in sharing details about her personal life, not only with those students sitting before her, but with her friends and co-workers in the town she had chosen to call home. While some people in the community where she practiced were aware that her father was a minister, especially those families of ministers for whom she provided free care, she revealed little additional information about her own family who lived hours away. Instead she surrounded herself with her patients and their histories, narrowing her own personal information to pictures framed and displayed on her desk. Yet, as in her patients' lives, family history significantly impacted the-who-she-was of Dr. Jane Carswell.

Her father, Arthur Dula Carswell, was cut from rugged pioneer mountain stock and independent Presbyterian theology. The Carswell family emigrated from Great Britain to Burke County, Georgia, moving inland from the port in Charleston around 1728. Before the American Revolution they migrated to western North Carolina's Burke County and settled there in the South Mountains. Jane's grandfather moved from the area into western Virginia in the late nineteenth century.

Arthur was born in Washington County, Virginia in January, 1888. He was raised in the mountainous surroundings of Abingdon, Virginia where he supported himself with several jobs, one of which included working as a salesman for RJ Reynolds Tobacco Company. He graduated from King College, a small private school sponsored by the Holston Presbytery in Bristol, Tennessee. He felt a call to the ministry and enrolled at Union Theological Seminary and Presbyterian School of Christian Education in Richmond, Virginia. He was licensed and ordained by the West Hanover Presbytery near Richmond where he served his first pastorate. He then answered the call to preach in the Cartersville, Virginia area in 1920.

On the other side of Jane's family, and on the opposite end of the state, the Warburton family on her mother's side traced its heritage to early settlers arriving from England in the Williamsburg and James City County area in 1642. An early ancestor of hers established *Pinewoods*, also known as the Warburton House, which still stands today and is part of the National Register of Historic Places.

Jane's mother, Madeline, was born in 1894. She suffered tragedy early in her life when her mother – Jane's grandmother Mary – was killed in a farm accident. Mary had been a devout follower of the Disciples of Christ, an ecumenical movement devoted to openness within Christian denominations. Though she died when her children were young, her influence over the development of their Christian faith lived on.

Madeline remained at her father's home helping with the younger children until she was sent to Williamsburg to live with her mother's brother, Edmund Ware Warburton, and his sister in order to finish her education. Neither this aunt nor the uncle had ever married, and both had remained living in the family home. Her uncle served for twelve years as the mayor of Williamsburg, beginning in 1904 and including those years when Madeline lived in the home as a part of the town's "first family."

The Warburton family home was later included in the restoration of Colonial Williamsburg and opened for viewing under the colonial owner's name, the Peyton Randolph House. This restoration began through the inspiration of Dr. William Goodwin, rector at Bruton Parish during the years Madeline attended the church with her aunt. He argued that the town's historical environment was being erased and he successfully pushed to restore the church in 1907. Financier John D. Rockefeller took up the cause and worked with him to establish a foundation to restore Williamsburg as an authentic colonial village.

After high school, Madeline attended Farmville Female Seminary Association's Institution, a small school in central Virginia mere miles from the scene of Lee's surrender to Grant at Appomattox. She worked in the YWCA at Farmville, attended churches of several denominations, and often told her family that "Morning Watch" and "Evening Prayers" were the most inspiring experiences of her college years. After she graduated, she was a teacher at what is now Mary

Washington University. There Jane's mother, Madeline Mapp Warburton, met her father, Rev. Arthur Dula Carswell.

By the beginning of 1923 Madeline was the lead teacher serving as both instructor and principal at a three-teacher high school in Cartersville, Virginia. She was a member of a Baptist church and taught Sunday School classes of young girls. Across town Arthur preached at a Presbyterian church. According to family lore, friction developed between a few members of the two congregations over a comment one of the Presbyterian elders made about a leading member of the Baptist church. Madeline went to Rev. Carswell to tell him of the potential of the conflict escalating. He attempted to be the peacemaker, but found it was not possible.

Madeline thought it was an impossible situation and that the only solution would be to leave. She approached him with the warning.

Arthur thought for a long moment and responded, "I'll leave if you'll go with me."

They went to a jeweler, purchased a ring, and married. She resigned her teaching job when an opportunity opened to start their new life away from Farmville, and in October of 1923 they left the potential danger of Virginia behind and moved, with uncertainty but in great faith, to Raeford, North Carolina.

2

Childhood

**"Mother and Daddy set an example for us
to ever be mindful of the needs of others."**
Jane Carswell, in a 2010 letter to nephew, David

 The small town of Raeford, North Carolina, located where the flat lands of the coastal plains gradually roll into sandhills, sat surrounded by longleaf pines that dripped their cones and needles and sap onto the grainy soil beneath them. In 1911 State Senator J. W. McLauchlin from Raeford sponsored a bill to create a new county, to be named Hoke County in honor of Confederate General Robert Frederick Hoke. The largely agrarian population of descendants of the Highland Scotts had immigrated and settled there before the American Revolution. McLauchlin recognized the need for a better system of roads to transport not only the wood from acres of forests, but the bales and bales of cotton from the white dotted fields. The flat, scrubby section of the county a few miles north of Raeford also provided isolation perfect for military training. Opened as Camp Bragg during the First World War, it reopened as a military base, Fort Bragg, a year before the Carswells arrived in the county.

This new calling for Rev. Carswell and his wife was preaching and ministering at a cluster of churches in Raeford, at the Bethel, Shiloh,

Philippi, and Dundarrach Presbyterian Churches and on fifth Sundays at Sandy Grove church (now a part of the Fort Bragg military base). Reverend Carswell soon became noted for his soft spoken, intellectual sermons that touched the hearts and minds of his congregations and as a result, the Carswells became not only leaders in their new community, but also the peacemakers. The family's housing was provided in town at a manse owned by the Presbytery and located near the home of two prominent citizens, J. W. McLauchlin, the state senator, and his wife, Christianna,. There Madeline easily adapted to being a pastor's wife. She went with her husband to all his churches but worked regularly in only one, the one nearest where they lived. She taught an adult Bible class in Sunday School and worked in several capacities in the Women of the Church auxiliary, most often as girls' Bible teacher. Although she had no formal training for church work, she had made up her mind early in life to do whatever she was asked in the church. She held to that resolution through the years of raising their seven children, all born during the years in Raeford. Jane,

Rev. Arthur Carswell

the middle child, arrived February 26, 1932. Her brother Arthur, Jr. and sisters Mary Thomas and Madeline, her mother's namesake, were older; her brother John and sisters Jill and Judy, younger. Her mother firmly believed that training the children to be faithful Christians was her most important task. She taught them compassion and integrity by living the example.

Madeline, Mary Thomas holding Jane, and Arthur

She altered clothing for the children that had been handed down not only from each other, but from well-meaning church members. She worked in the garden where they raised their own vegetables she shared with those people from the community who were "in need." Meanwhile, her husband was often paid, "in kind" with an offering of produce from other people's gardens or meat from a butchering. The children witnessed their family helping others when they helped deliver picnic baskets of food for those sick or hungry.

The family moved to Sanford January 3, 1940, when her father assumed the duties of pastor at Buffalo, White Hill, Pocket, Euphronia Presbyterian Churches, and The Church in the Horseshoe on fifth Sundays. According to Jane's recollection years later, the ground was covered with snow and topped with a layer of ice on the day they moved into the manse at Buffalo. Shortly after settling in, they were warmly greeted with poundings from members of the four churches in the charge: a pound of flour, sugar, coffee, lard, cornmeal, or a country ham with canned vegetables or jams and jellies. Her father's total salary from the four churches was one thousand, five hundred dollars per year. The congregation, most of whom didn't earn that much money, was very generous with what they did have.

The manse lacked the promised indoor bathroom when they first arrived, so they used a two-seater privy out back. As the majority of members of the community and the church itself had the same type accommodations, church members did not see why their minister insisted that the promised indoor bathroom be installed. Nearly eight weeks after they arrived, the family finally had indoor plumbing.

Like most homes of that era there was no central heat. A large stove was located in the living room, and to the delight of the younger children in the family there was a hot air register in the ceiling of the living room which opened into a bedroom upstairs. On special occasions, such as weddings in the manse, they could view the goings-on from above without being seen. The Women's Circles frequently met there. One of the visiting ladies got the idea that while they were there "they ought to check the house out to see if any repairs were needed." Jane's mother did not encourage this, but they proceeded with their inspection. Her brother, Arthur D., by then a teenager, was not the tidiest person in the world but was talented in electrical matters. He had wired his door knob to an electric current to keep his little brother and sisters out of his belongings. The good ladies got a shock in more ways than one when they opened the door to his room.

To celebrate birthdays, their mother dressed them in their finest clothes for the yearly photograph. Each child, without fail, received a birthday cake served with custard-like homemade ice cream from a family recipe that Jane held onto and used throughout her life.

Jane was nine years old on Pearl Harbor Day, December 7, 1941. She did not fully understand what was going on when people spoke in whispers. She only knew that something terrible had happened. Jane's mother was an inveterate letter writer who corresponded with the boys from the congregation who were away in service during the war. The congregation was filled with sadness as a gold star went on the service banner at church when a church member was lost at sea. There were many weddings on short notice as servicemen shipped overseas, most taking place at the manse. On one occasion the marriage license had been obtained in an adjoining county, so to make the marriage legal, the wedding party proceeded at night to a bridge on the county line and held the ceremony by headlights of their cars.

Her brother Arthur was the prankster of the family. He invented a "lie detector machine" that he used to his advantage against his brothers and sisters. He told their brother John that if he didn't let him wash his ears (his chore was to give him a bath), that corn kernels would grow into cornstalks in his ears with all the dirt in them. He put his sister Mary Thomas' new pocketbook out by the highway in front of the house and tied it on a string that he would jerk out from under anyone who would stop to pick it up. The girls in the family created an uproar when someone stepped on the string, broke it, and made off with the purse. Once Arthur told Jane there were little people in the radio talking and that the static was miniature lions roaring. Jane related this at school and the teacher put on her report card that she had a "great imagination."

Arthur taught Jane how to play baseball, although she usually pitched or played outfield while he batted. Unknown to Arthur, Jane learned to ride a bicycle using his bike. She and her sister Madeline would "borrow" it while he wasn't home and practice on it. The bent frame happened when one of them was going down the hill to the mailbox and ran into the tree in the curve. He also introduced Jane to golf when he gave her a wooden putter for her birthday one year.

At Christmas, in addition to her regular cooking, Jane's mother made large amounts of candy, cookies, and fruitcake. She did all the Christmas shopping for the family and wrote all the cards. On Christmas Eve, Jane's mother went outside their house and rang bells under the window, hoping the children would think it was Santa Claus, her way to get the children in bed. As the preacher's wife, she also was in charge of the Christmas pageants with the manger scene, shepherds, angels, and wise men. Once during the war when there were few males available to act, Jane was a wise man. On Christmas nights the congregation gathered at the church not only for the pageant but also for the arrival of Santa Claus. The brown bags that Santa gave out were filled with hard candy, an orange, an apple, raisins, nuts and if the year was prosperous, with a tangerine as well. One Christmas everyone in the family

was sick except Jill and Mary Thomas, who by default, became the two who had to find and cut the Christmas tree. They returned from the cow pasture with a huge cedar tree that was about four feet too tall for the living room. Jane's parents joked about letting it extend up through the register to the upstairs.

Vacation Bible School was organized by Jane's mother who, like many ministers' wives in small churches at that time, was the unpaid Director of Christian Education. She traveled into the byways and hedges and rounded up children. The school lasted two weeks, with cookies and punch served the last day. An event the children looked forward to each day was the Bible story hour when all classes came together to learn about the heroes of the Bible. They seemed especially fond of the violent stories in the Old Testament such as Samson, David and Goliath, and Jezebel's gory death. They studied the Child's and Shorter Catechisms, memorized scripture, and learned the books of the Bible. Reciting the catechisms to teacher, Miss Charley King, was greatly motivated by the fact that Mr. Belk of Belk Department Stores awarded anyone with a dollar for reciting the Child's and five dollars for the Shorter, which was actually quite long with over a hundred questions and answers. As the Carswell children grew older they helped teach in weekly Sunday Schools and yearly Bible Schools.

Several dogs attended Bible School one summer and frequently came inside where the temperature was cooler. A week or two after school ended there seemed to be an epidemic of church members scratching their ankles and lower legs. Fleas were discovered, and an exterminator was called in. Another summer a group of the young people made marionettes and wrote and planned to present a play of the book of Esther. The production was set for the woodhouse behind the manse. The marionettes' hair was made of corn silk, and the rats in the woodhouse took a liking to it. The day before the performance several of the puppets were found to be bald.

With seven children in the manse there was a large and active youth group, the Young Peoples' League. Halloween and Tacky parties and other "Socials" were held at the community club house, a small building in the woods between the church and town. The leader made sure the children did mission work. At least once a year they visited an invalid member of the church. The walk to her home was three miles through the woods. After arriving, the youth members recited Bible verses and sang, accompanied by an old pump organ in the room played by Jane's sister Madeline. A major problem was that her legs were too short to reach the pedals to pump it. Jane's job was to crawl under the piano bench and pump the pedals. Jane wrote that their songs were joyful but not too melodic and added, "Fortunately the lady was hard of hearing."

They attended Youth Conference at Peace College in Raleigh. To earn money for tuition, the young people sold homemade ice cream at the Curb Market in Sanford, an early form of a Farmer's Market. One of the biggest thrills of attending Conference was riding the train to Raleigh. When they exited the train, rather than going directly to the college, they trudged with their suitcases to a boarding house, where they ate well before they walked on to the college.

Jane in a Chinese Outfit given to her by the McLauchlin's

Of her growing up years, Jane recognized the perspective that shaped her, "watching others who believe in God is the easiest way to start believing in God yourself." She first declared her intention to become a doctor when she was four years old. The family neighbors, the McLauchlins who lived nearby in Raeford, had intrigued her with stories of her surgeon brother, Dr. Archibald McFayden and his mission in China. He returned on leave from the medical mission field telling Jane stories about being a doctor. He was present in China during the Japanese invasion in World War II where his mission compound sheltered refugees and returned to the states in 1942 as a part of the prisoner-of-war exchange.

Jane's dream to become a physician became stronger as she grew older. She overheard a conversation one day among several boys in her junior high class bragging they were going to medical school. She inserted that she was too, and they responded, "You can't do that. You're a girl." She took that as a challenge. She was poor. She was a girl. But she was determined.

Living in a preacher's family both during the Great Depression and during the rationing of the war years meant stretching already limited resources even further and sharing them with others whenever possible. When Jane was around thirteen years old, she and her sister Madeline took the job of cleaning the church for three dollars a month. Every three months or so her mother helped to see that the church got a thorough cleaning. As she grew older, Jane was in great demand to pick cotton for a penny a pound in the fields surrounding their home. Likewise, her reputation as a stringer in the tobacco fields was well known. She was so quick she could work with two handers at a time as she tied the leaves onto the sticks to be cured. At home, her mother chose her to pick pecans from their shells for her Christmas baking because Jane didn't like the untoasted ones and wouldn't eat them as she worked.

In 1948 the family once again packed up their seven children, several cats, a dog, and the cow and moved this time to Manchester, North Carolina when her father became the pastor of the Church of the Covenant, Cameron Hill and Cypress Presbyterian Churches in Spring Lake. Because Rev. Carswell had several different congregations, his schedule varied from Sunday to Sunday, yet one thing was constant. No matter where he was stationed, or where he preached, someone in the congregation always invited him and his family to Sunday dinner. He was a pleasant guest, a good conversationalist and as well informed on world affairs as he was on the gospel.

During her freshman and sophomore years of high school, Jane attended Sanford High School, but with the family's move to a new community, she attended Anderson Creek High School her junior and senior years. She was captain and high scorer on the girls' basketball team where she delighted in telling about an incident that happened one day on the court.

A fan for the opposing side screamed at her each time she had the ball, but she didn't understand what he his words. During a time-out she asked the coach what the man was saying.

"Replant."

"Replant?"

"Yes," the coach said. "He's a farmer and he's insulting you by calling you a replant." Being from an agrarian community, Jane knew

exactly what the insult meant. She was like the replanted crop in the flood or hail damaged acreage of a field, short and not as worthy as the first plants. Jane, however, proved to be worthy. She graduated class Valedictorian, 1950.

Each of the children grew into upstanding citizens of their

respective communities and in the professions they chose. As brothers and sisters they shared distinct personality traits with Jane, according to her nephew, Robert Carswell. Arthur Dula, Junior, named for his father, worked as an inspector at a Fasco factory in Fayetteville, North Carolina. He had the same sense of wonder and traveling that Jane relished in her life.

Her oldest sister, Mary Thomas (Helwig) taught high school science in Cleveland, Ohio. Like Jane, Mary Thomas was a prolific volunteer, setting up the first library and an adult literacy center in Providence Forge, Virginia. Madeline Mapp, named for her mother, lived at home and taught first grade. She had the same gift as Jane to connect personally with people of all walks of life. Jane always wanted to be a physician, but did substitute teach for one day. Unlike her mother and these sisters who found their passion in teaching, Jane never returned to teach in a classroom.

Jane with her sister Jill and husband Hal Wallof

Her younger brother John worked in the social security office in Richmond, Virginia. Like Jane he had a deep sense of right and wrong, living without contradictions and being generous to those in need. Jane's sister, Virgilia (Wallof), or Jill as she was known, was a pharmacist at Duke Hospital Pharmacy in Durham, North Carolina. Like Jane, she was very studious in her schooling, extremely inviting, and had a deep love of the outdoors. The baby of the family, Judy Avent, was bookkeeper for a construction firm in Lumberton, North Carolina. She was similar to Jane in that she was fun, playful, and had a deep bond to North Carolina.

Jane with her brother John Carswell and wife Betty

"The culmination of all these attributes resided in Jane's character throughout her life," her nephew Robert added. Jane enjoyed her family, and Robert and his brother marveled at the many letters that generation exchanged over the years. He went on to say about her influence, "There is just a weakness of words and too many memories to try and continue to describe Aunt Jane. That was because she was a woman of action who knew Christianity was in the details, details that were thankless and mundane yet helped so many people. She helped give me perspective and framed some of my most fundamental beliefs growing up."

Jane's father retired from the ministry in 1958, and he and her mother moved to Providence Forge, Virginia where she died in 1973 and he died in 1976.

Arthur and Madeline Carswell

3

College

"Those first two years at Flora Macdonald were a very
steadying influence on my first experience away from home."
Jane Carswell in the *Sandhills Citizen*
December 12, 1984

The Highland Scots had brought to the new world along with their Presbyterian faith, a love of learning and a strong commitment to the education of their children, boys and girls alike. Originally, they founded Floral College a few miles west of the small community of Red Springs in the sandhills of North Carolina. Opened from 1841 through 1878, it held the distinction as the first school in North Carolina to award diplomas to women. The Cape Fear Presbytery in 1896 established Red Springs Seminary near Floral College. In 1903 the school became known as the Southern Presbyterian College and Conservatory of Music until it received its final name in 1915, Flora Macdonald College, in honor of a local heroine.

Those Scots who settled in the sandhills of North Carolina during the American colonial period left their homeland seeking a life away from the politics and strife their country had just endured. Among immigrants this new life attracted was a person of note, Flora Macdonald. Earlier, in 1745 Charles Edward Stuart arrived in Scotland from France to campaign for the British crown that he felt was his by lineage. Known as the "Pretender Prince" or as Bonny Prince Charlie, (especially to later generations of grade school children studying North Carolina social studies), he amassed an army against the rightful heir, the Duke of Cumberland, stormed through Edinburgh and battled toward London, until his troops had no option but to retreat. He fled and hid in the hills and caves of Scotland with a bounty on his head, dead or alive. Anyone sheltering him would be killed.

His salvation came from a young Scot, Flora Macdonald, and a grand plot for her to travel home to the Isle of Skye. She arranged passage aboard a boat to transport both her and the prince disguised as a maid. They were fired upon, but escaped, and the prince fled. The authorities learned of her part in the tyranny and arrested her, but the rebellion had been squelched, the future throne of the Duke of Cumberland saved, and with no more threat, she was pardoned.

She and her husband were among the many who later chose to leave Scotland and the turmoil behind. Before they sailed, however, they were required to pledge an oath of loyalty to the British government. They arrived in North Carolina in 1774 only to find themselves embroiled in the politics of independence. With her notoriety as leverage, Flora Macdonald reminded the North Carolina Scots of their oath and pled that they fight for the crown against these colonial insurrectionists. Her husband and son were captured by the Continental Army at the Battle of Moore's Creek Bridge in the Carolina coastal plains, imprisoned and later released in Canada. Flora returned to the Isle of Skye after the American War for Independence where her family eventually joined her. Although she no longer lived in America, tales of her loyalty and steadfastness in the face of danger long survived her stay. In tribute to her virtues, and to maintain a link between those descendants in America with a Scottish heritage and their European roots, the school received the name, Flora Macdonald.

Rev. and Mrs. Arthur Carswell were among the many Presbyterians who entrusted their daughters' safety and post high school upbringing to this school. Designed to educate young women not only in book knowledge, but also in the social graces demanded of women in the twentieth century, Flora Macdonald College (Flossie Mac to those young women in its care) met the challenge through a structured atmosphere and a liberal arts curriculum. It trained them in the service of the Lord and encouraged them to grow in their Christian faith.

As the first-born daughter, Mary Thomas had been the one who benefited from her family's scrimping and sacrificing to pay her tuition and expenses. She attended North Carolina's Women's College in Greensboro realizing she would deplete most of the savings and therefore would be expected to contribute money to pay the tuition for the next sister in line, Madeline, who chose to attend Flora Macdonald. In turn when Madeline graduated, she was expected to contribute money for Jane's school tuition, and then Jane to help the next sister in line as well.

Flora Macdonald College showing the dome on top

As her sisters ahead of her had done, Jane supplemented the tuition money in a variety of ways. She picked cotton in the hot southern humidity, tied tobacco leaves on splintery racks to be hung and cured in the barns, and cleaned the churches where her father was pastor. Her main task as janitor at one of her father's churches was to build fires. She was the high school representative to the Sanford newspaper, the *Herald*, where she was paid by the inch of print, and where she learned to expand her articles with extra words. She entered a Stewardship Essay Contest through the General Council of the Presbyterian Church and won a twenty-five dollar, third place award and a commendation for her "fine work in living and teaching the principles of stewardship."

She was no stranger to the Flora Macdonald campus at the far end of the Red Springs community. Jane had walked through the formal parlors at the main entrance and sat in their stuffed divans situated beneath portraits of the namesake and the school's founders while she waited for her sister, Madeline. A rich brown elegance of oak paneled walls and floors greeted her and other visitors in the foyer and the reception hall of the main floor rotunda. With the exception of a few utility buildings, a gymnasium, and a tiny swimming pool lovingly called the Tea Cup, the entire school was located in one massive structure dominated in the center by a dome towering above a four story high rotunda. Majestic columns on the front exterior overlooked gardens and a graceful fountain, where after the supper meal, the students liked to meet. The conservatory was graced with a pipe organ in the auditorium. Dr. Wadell, the original founder from 1896, was still living when Jane attended school there, and although he was aged, he spoke every week at the required Wednesday chapel services held in the auditorium.

Second floor rotunda

It was also the scene each Friday of a concert or lecture series. The students dressed in evening gowns and met each visiting artist. Bennet Cerf, the noted humorist, wrote in his column that he had been at Flora Macdonald College where the cream of southern womanhood attend.

Years later Jane wrote a tongue-in-cheek description of her preparations and packing to go away to college:

HOW TO BE A FASHION PLATE
AT FLORA MACDONALD COLLEGE IN 1950

Straight out of high school in 1950
I was headed for college and wished to look nifty.
To furnish my wardrobe so I'd look nice
A '49 annual offered fashion advice.
Saddle shoes, bobby sox were all the rage,
Short sleeved sweaters were on every page.
Little square scarves were around most necks
Or a Peter Pan collar, what the heck?
For a broomstick skirt I saved feed sacks.
It cost a lot less than clothes off the racks.
The length of skirts was just mid-calf,
And a suit for Sunday I'd have to have
With matching gloves and also a hat
And heels I could walk in. Imagine that!
Some mornings for breakfast you'd need, please note,
To hide your pajamas, a long raincoat.
To jump in the Tea Cup, a demure swim suit
With a prim little skirt, it was really a hoot.
For frequent recitals, have an evening dress
With puffed sleeves and crinolines to look your best.
When I looked at pictures of the blue gym suit
With little bitty bloomers, I knew I'd look cute.
To wear kilts for the fling would really be fun.
I'd dance my best in the May Day sun.
Some girls had plaids from the family clan,
With my family's budget, that wasn't my plan.
McCrory's Dime Store furnished the plaid.
My mother stitched it up, and it didn't look bad.
I packed hair rollers to use each night.
Straight hair in the '50's was a terrible sight.
My family all helped my clothes to pack
And wished me well at Flossie Mac.

One of the most important items Jane packed when she was first leaving for school was the kilt her mother had sewn for her. Each class was assigned a different color, theirs was blue. During their freshmen year the girls were required to learn the Highland Fling in their physical education class. Decades later, when Jane was over seventy years old, she astonished a group of friends one day at a musical gathering when she broke into a lively Highland Fling.

Photograph Courtesy of Flora Macdonald Legacy Board

Highland Fling photograph from the May 7, 1946
Flora Macdonald College Semicentennial Celebration
program booklet, before Jane's arrival on campus.

Academic classes met on the first floor of the building. Dormitory rooms were located on the second and third floors. Jane was assigned a room on West Third during her two years at the school. Before the school added private mail boxes later in Jane's first year, the student who had the post office scholarship stood on the top story of the rotunda and dropped letters over the bannister to the girls waiting below.

During Jane's freshman year she played intramural basketball and hit the winning shot when the freshmen defeated the seniors in the tournament. She wrote of a tradition at the school:

MASCOT MADNESS

In the days when Flora Macdonald College existed there was little in the way of entertainment in the town of Red Springs. Consequently the students created their own activities.

Intramural sports were big events featuring basketball, volleyball, and earlier field hockey. Freshmen, sophomores, juniors, and seniors competed against each other with great vigor and spirit. Each class also had a mascot, which was one of four stuffed animals. The only ones which I remember were the bulldog and the tiger. Upon graduation, that class's mascot was passed down to the incoming freshman class. The mascots were to be present at each game, and if not present at the final game of the tournament, although its team beat all the others, that class could not "really" be said to be the winner.

Because of this unwritten rule, mascots were frequently stolen and hidden from their rightful owners. Much ingenuity was used in finding secure hiding places both to protect your own mascot and those secreted away from other classes. Sometimes pillows were opened, part of the contents removed, the mascot stuffed inside, and then sewed up again. The school nurse, Miss Connor, was known to have cloistered mascots in the infirmary.

One memorable night I snuck out during study hour to bury the class of 1954's bulldog in the gardens. He was securely wrapped to keep out moisture, and I crept out after dark. I had dug a hole under some azaleas and had gotten it covered up when I saw a flashlight approaching through the dark. The bearer of the light turned out to be one of the student council members. She sternly asked what I was doing out of my room during study hour, and I feared the worst. With quick thinking I replied, "Why, I have one night out a month because of my grades, and I decided to spend it out here. Is there anything wrong with that?"

I don't remember her reply, but I quickly ended my night out and got back to my room. I fully expected to be called before the student council but never heard anything more about it. Years later, I found out that the senior student council member, Jan Williamson, who almost caught me in the act, was also out in the gardens planning to hide her class mascot.

We actually won the basketball tournament that year, and had our bulldog present at the final game. This banner also hung in the gym during all of our games. Alas, the fate of the actual bulldog is not known.

Red Springs was named for a stream of water where the iron content was high and the water ran red, so red that the tubs at school were stained. Jane's sophomore year, the girls performed a skit for the incoming freshman class. A red haired girl in their class wrapped a towel around her head and came out of "taking a bath and shampooing her hair." She dramatically pulled the towel away and screamed, "Oh, look what's happened to my hair. It's turning red!"

Jane was in the choral club that traveled to various churches for concerts. She was active in her prayer band, a part of the Student Christian Association. She was a member of the student volunteers, a group involved with mission studies and who taught Bible lessons to the black students in their school in Red Springs. She excelled in creative writing, joined the Writer's Club, and was on the staff of the college magazine, *The Pine and Thistle*. She was a member of the Mathematical Honor Society, the William Bartram Scientific Society, and served as Vice President of the freshman class.

On Sunday mornings, Jane, along with the other freshmen, were required to dress in their finest hats, white gloves, and stockings, and walk, in heels, a fairly long distance from the portico, down the steps, down the driveway and the road, to the Presbyterian church for Sunday School and morning services. No one seemed to mind until once, when the pouring rain emboldened them to dare beg Mrs. McCain, the Dean of Women, to allow them to forgo wearing hats that one morning. She folded her arms across her chest, leaned forward and said to the unfortunate delegate before her, "My dear young lady, you are ladies and you will wear your hats to church."

After the long walk back to the school, Mrs. McCain would ring the large dinner gong and have the blessing. The dining room scholarship students (table girls) served the Sunday dinner family style as they did every other meal, three times a day. After dinner the girls rested, walked in the gardens, studied, and often visited with dates. Then followed another walk to the Red Springs Church for Westminister Fellowship and back to the campus for a bag supper. The cooks had Sunday afternoons off.

Sunday evenings were filled with hymn sings. Those girls with dates sat on the first floor in the reception area of the rotunda. All others gathered in the circle surrounding the rotunda on the second and third floors and sang to the accompaniment of the piano on the first floor. After the sings, Jane attended the Sunday evening meditations in the auditorium. One final weekend activity, she gathered her laundry into her laundry bag labeled with her name, took it to the unused elevator shaft, and dropped it in. Later in the week, she went by the laundry and picked it up.

Mondays were designated as travel days for those who had gone home over the weekend. Riding in a car during school was forbidden, unless the student was with a family member or had obtained special permission. There were in and out cards to sign any time they left. They were allowed to go into Red Springs on Saturday morning, but were required to return to campus by lunchtime, before the locals arrived in town. They participated in community activities, especially those sponsored by the Presbyterian Church. They had a float in the Christmas parade featuring the May queen. Birthdays were celebrated on Wednesday nights with cakes and a special dinner cooked by the kitchen staff.

Movies were not necessarily a regular part of Jane's life, however, there was a theater in town and she occasionally went to special movies. This theater had three entrances, one for the whites, one for blacks, and one for the members of the Native American Lumbee tribe.

Girls were allowed to date, mostly on weekends, but for their safety, and the school's reputation, they had to remain on campus during the date. Red Springs was a half hour drive from the Fort Bragg military base, and often a girl had a date with a soldier who brought friends with him. An announcement would come over the speaker, "Anybody want a date?" Most of these soldiers were heading to battle in the Korean War.

Jane had been on the Dean's List each grading period since her arrival. She was a dedicated, hardworking student who her friends found, always had a precious sense of humor. She endeared herself to her classmates as well as to the faculty. The professors were interested in all their pupils, and with a total of just over three hundred students enrolled in the entire school, spent quality time in small class sizes and with them as individuals. Jane was a favorite of chemistry professor, Dr. Glenn, who became a mentor to her and encouraged her in her career choice. She planned to retire at the end of Jane's sophomore year and would no longer be a part of the faculty. Knowing of Jane's dreams for medical school, Dr. Glenn recommended that she leave Flora Macdonald College because of its limited science curriculum. In the fall of 1952 Jane followed her mentor's counsel and left the protected environment at Flora Macdonald to enroll at the University of North Carolina at Chapel Hill.

Years later, the Alumni Council of St. Andrews Presbyterian College in Laurinburg, North Carolina, the school that opened in 1961 when Flora Macdonald merged with Presbyterian Junior College, presented their 1997 distinguished Alumni Award to Jane Carswell in recognition of her caring dedication to her church, her profession, and her community. In 2014 Jane created an annual scholarship at the school in memory of her sister Madeline Carswell and her brother Arthur D. Carswell, with preference given to a major in elementary education or religious work.

Jane developed friendships at Flora Macdonald that continued throughout her life, a special bond bringing them together at frequent reunions and mountain retreats where Jane's classmates reminisced about their years together. Much of the conversation between classmates Saradee (Dee) Davis Bowen. Dehanie Boncy Goldston, Norma Jean Thompson Price, and Mary Sue Coleman Jones Jessick is written above.

Jane, third from left on first row,
with her friends at a Flora Macdonald reunion

4

University

*"I was raised in a family and a church
that made me want to go into a helping profession."*
Jane Carswell in the *Raleigh News and Observer*
December 13, 1984

Transferring from an all girls' school with a population of three hundred into a male dominated school of thousands presented Jane with a new set of challenges. The student population at the University of North Carolina at Chapel Hill was overwhelmingly men, despite the fact it had graduated the first woman in 1898, slightly over a half century before Jane's arrival.

She could not have enrolled at the university any earlier in her college career, because at that time women were not accepted as freshmen or sophomores. That progress happened in 1963, nearly a dozen years too late for Jane. For women, the freshman year choices were limited to Greensboro's state supported Women's College or any of several junior colleges specifically designed to prepare graduates for their final two years at Carolina. Or, as in Jane's case, women could attend a wide variety of church sponsored schools, like Flora Macdonald, for which she was most thankful. She often stated she would not have done her schooling any other way.

From the intimate sized classes in her previous school, she found herself in auditorium sized classes with one hundred plus other students, mostly men, taught by men. As the custom called for in those years, professors addressed students using their surnames. Carswell. In one class she consistently distinguished herself with high scores on tests. While his two graduate assistants returned tests and papers to the hundred plus students, this particular professor announced the highest score. Jane typically earned that distinction, yet he always called her "Mr." Carswell. The entire term he never recognized her gender.

She found a kindred soul in her new roommate, Franke Bell, the one with an added "e" to feminize the name. Their room was on the third floor of Carr, a dormitory built in 1900, named in honor of the man who donated the money to build it, a tobacco magnate of Bull Durham fame. It was drab, falling apart, and nothing like the elegance of the mellow oak wood of her previous environment.

By their second year, they had added two more roommates and had taken over a double bunk suite in the back corner of the third floor. This bunk room came with a smaller room to the side with desks for studying. During that time she and Franke both loved the book, *Winnie the Pooh* and its main character, the lovable, bumbling Pooh. Since Jane was a tiny person, barely over a hundred pounds, petite in build, much smaller than Franke, she took on the persona of Piglet, the one who straightened out Pooh, and Franke became Pooh, "Franke the Pooh." They posted a sign, "Pooh Corner" on their door. Jane was serious, but she had a good sense of humor as the roommates laughed through their Pooh days. They studied together, ate in the cafeteria together, and played tennis against each other on weekends, with Jane usually victorious. Carolina wasn't all play for either of them. Jane had a heavy class pre-med load and studied almost constantly. Franke worked three jobs in addition to her studies. On Sundays Jane worshiped at a Presbyterian church while Franke went with one of the other roommates to various churches.

Jane rarely went home on weekends, unlike many students in the suitcase college town of Chapel Hill who out of boredom, or job necessity, usually left town on non-football game Saturdays. One unforgettable day, however, she was called home when her youngest sister Judy was critically ill with rheumatic fever. Their father met Jane at the bus station in Fayetteville. Rev. Arthur D. Carswell was not a man to show or even talk about his emotions, but Jane never forgot that one time at the bus station when he wished it were he who was sick instead of his daughter, that he was at the end of his life and she had such a bright future ahead. Jane went on to say she thought that everyone in the family would have taken the illness from Judy if they could have. Thankfully she recovered.

Her brother John was also a student in Chapel Hill, but the two of them were busy with their own friends and studies, and rarely saw each other. As her senior year was ending, Jane worried about the pledge she had made, the promise that she would graduate and get a job and pay tuition for the next sister in line, just like her sisters had done for her. Jill, however, told her to go ahead to medical school, that she could go to college any time. Jill followed through with that statement and eventually did further her education to become a pharmacist.

With the knowledge that she was now financially able to follow her dream, Jane applied simultaneously to medical school at the University of North Carolina and the Medical College of Virginia in Richmond, not all that far from her mother's family. Her grades were high, better than most, and she was graduating Phi Beta Kappa near the top of her class. She would earn not only academic distinctions, but athletic as well, being recognized by the Women's Athletic Association as the most outstanding girl athlete in the class of 1954. The dorm where she lived won honors as the leading female dorm in athletic intramural competition, thanks in part to Jane's prowess.

In 1954 she heard from her application to the medical school at Carolina.

Rejected.

She was disappointed, not devastated. Her faith was so strong that she firmly believed God had a better plan for her. She had not heard from Richmond and there was still hope. When that letter arrived in the post box shared by the girls in the suite, Jane was on the other side of campus, and Franke found the letter first. It sat unopened in its place, and Franke sat worried. Finally, Jane opened the letter.

Accepted. To the Medical College of Virginia in Richmond.

Then word arrived from Carolina. Although she had not appealed her rejection, the committee had reconsidered, and she was now accepted. Their reason for denying her entrance was a doubt in her physical ability to withstand the stresses of their program, considering her petite size. She appeared too frail.

She went to Richmond.

So did Franke, to work and live with her aunt and uncle. Despite their plans, they saw little of each other with Jane's classes and then her residency consuming all her time. Once on their rare chance to meet, out of curiosity Franke asked a strange question. "Are there many women who have the baby before they get to the delivery room?"

"There are more little children running around Richmond with the middle name Otis than you would ever believe," Jane replied with a bit of droll medical humor in reference to the inventor of the elevator.

Colonial Studios of Richmond
Jane's 1958 MCV Yearbook Picture

For her specialty, she chose the field she felt was the discipline that meshed her goals with her personality - general practice. She wanted to be on the front lines of an individual's medical care, working alongside the patient, diagnosing, advising, and practically becoming an extended member of each family. She would be expected to be proficient in obstetrics and gynecology, pediatrics, psychiatry, internal medicine, surgery and community medicine.

Four other women were in the class, giving them five strong to support each other. They navigated the big city streets outside and the male dominated hospital rounds inside. When the occasional hostility was directed at the women, they all learned to develop a tough shell.

They even heard whispers about the men complaining the women were favored. All five women finished the program.

During the summer of 1957, Jane worked at Rex Hospital in Raleigh, North Carolina. This gave her not only an income, but supervised experience practicing medicine. Nursing supervisor at the time, Suggie Styres, reports that Jane was well liked by staff and patients, and as she rotated through the various areas in the hospital, was impressive. "It was obvious then that she took care of details."

Jane distinguished herself at the Medical College of Virginia and was initiated into the Alpha Omega Alpha Honor Medical Society. She became noted as a diagnostician who typically inquired about the patient's family situation. In June, 1958 the American Medical Women's Association, Inc. awarded her an honorable mention citation in recognition of her "outstanding scholastic record." During its traditional banquet at a Richmond country club, the Medical College of Virginia recognized her for placing among the top ten 1958 graduates. Thrilled to have earned her spot, Jane dressed for the occasion and appeared as directed at the clubhouse, only to be redirected to the side door. Women were not members of the club and therefore, no woman was allowed to enter through the front. When a female friend of hers won the same honor two years later, Jane had prepared her. She entered in the front door.

Jane completed a rotating internship at the Medical College of Virginia in 1959. She followed that with a family practice residency in Richmond with Dr. Kinlock Nelson, finishing in 1960.

With medical school, a one-year internship and a year in residency in general practice now completed, Doctor Jane Triplett Carswell, Family Physician, was finally ready for her first professional job.

In 2008 the surviving four met for a fifty year reunion

All five women in the Medical College of Virginia's class of 1958 had successful careers in medicine.

In addition to Jane,
Louisa Satchwell Batman
Jeanne Plunkett Beckett
Beverly Noe Chambers
Vivian Myrtle Wilkerson

5

Kentucky

"Dear God, Thank you for giving us all skills and talents.
Help us to use them in good ways so that other people will
come to know Jesus and His love
and how He wants us to live. Amen."
From "God Given Talents"
Jane Carswell, 2001

 Four hundred miles and a universe away from her life in Richmond was the mining town of Lynch, Kentucky, and a possible option for Dr. Jane Carswell's first job out of residency. She was looking for a position in a small town. She wanted families to serve, a place where she could practice her faith as much as practice her medicine.

She found what she was looking for.

She pictured Lynch as the answer to this small town her mind had envisioned. It was a world away from all she was accustomed to, an isolated entity tucked deep in Harlan County's coalfields. West of Richmond and Chapel Hill and Raeford and all places she called familiar, the town was located not all that far from the Virginia border. A plus, she found, it was less than a hundred miles from Abingdon, the western Virginia town where her father was born, where she had a connection, and even closer to where her father had gone to college in Bristol, Tennessee. The sandhills of her childhood now gave way to towering Appalachian cliffs. The city traffic of Richmond became only memories with her car navigating mountain curves. She was ready to leave the tidewater of the last few years and venture into a new life. She was equipped with the integrity and compassion her parents instilled in her as a young child, coupled with the knowledge and skill from her medical school training.

Lynch, Kentucky had a heritage unlike any Jane had experienced. It was a created town from its very inception, something made out of nothing in a matter of months. In 1917, World War I was winding down and the economy was revving up. The United States Steel Corporation needed coal for fuel to power furnaces used in the steel smelting process. Realizing coal mines in eastern Kentucky had already proved themselves to be productive, US Steel, as it was known, purchased acres of land along a back road in the Kentucky hills to develop a mining operation.

However the enormity of the task ahead involved more than digging a hole in the side of the mountain. Thousands of miners needed to be hired, but housing them would overwhelm the nearest town of Cumberland, a mere five miles away. A call for more and more miners resulted in the arrival of hard working immigrants from across the world bringing with them a variety of nationalities, races, cultures and beliefs. At its peak, the population of Lynch was around ten thousand, essentially all employed in some capacity by US Steel. Every element that made a town into a town was created from the ground up in Lynch. The company built homes where only those employed by US Steel were eligible to live. Should a miner or other worker be fired or injured beyond returning, the house had to be vacated to make room for a waiting family. The company built a grand hotel for temporary shelter when the demand for houses exceeded the availability. It built schools for the miners' children, a movie theater, and a store for families to shop for food and clothing. With no competition, prices in the store were often higher than those in surrounding communities. Workers in those enterprises were employees of the company as well and were held to the same housing requirements. On payday, rent and accumulated charges at the company store were deducted from the earnings. Miners and other employees alike were obligated to remain on the job until any debt they owed was paid. Also deducted was a required fee, a dollar or two in the early years, for individual and family health care supplied by US Steel.

The hospital where Dr. Jane Carswell later worked was built in 1920 and, like the remainder of the town's citizens, the physicians and nurses were company employees. The hospital existed through the years of the miners' backbreaking successes in discovering rich veins, and through their injuries and deaths from accidents or unexpected cave-ins. When the United Mine Workers attempted to unionize the Lynch miners, the hospital was there to handle injuries from ensuing violence. When disagreements between workers and management escalated into what became known as Bloody Harlan, the hospital assisted.

The hospital was also there as better equipment increased output in the mines, and lessened injuries. Because each new machine replaced twenty or more miners, an exodus of displaced and laid off workers reduced the town's population by the thousands. Yet the hospital maintained a presence as a necessary element of the town.

By 1950 the United States Coal and Coke Company had taken over operation of the mining business and made the decision to sell Lynch Hospital to the Sisters of Notre Dame, a Catholic order in Covington, Kentucky. The sisters paid the asking price of one dollar for the building and all its equipment and materials on hand at the December thirty-first transition. However, mineral rights from under the hospital were retained by the company. If any damage to the building occurred in the process of mining beneath the hospital, the company was not liable. The Catholic bishop, the Most Reverend William Mulloy, agreed to the terms. The annals of the order lists the reason behind the purchase: to expand into the rural areas with the desire "to bring Christ to the crossroads of Kentucky."

Photo contributed by MaryJo O'Bradovich
Lynch's Notre Dame Hospital

As an extension of the terms, the head physician, Dr. Leland Payton agreed to run a medical practice under his jurisdiction and be Chief of Staff at what was now named Notre Dame Hospital. US Coal and Coke retained the ambulance service, however, since it was primarily used for transporting injured employees.

In all, nine sisters were working at the hospital by the time Jane arrived in 1960. Many of the patients were former miners suffering from what became known as black lung, the chronic disease developed from breathing years upon years of coal dust. As a family physician, Jane also delivered babies and doctored the sick. When she was recognized as the National Family Physician of the Year in 1984, she received a congratulatory letter from former a colleague, Dr. James Gibson, commenting, "I was glad when you arrived [in Lynch] since you had had a little bit more experience in breech deliveries than I had had."

Of the dozen or so doctors affiliated with the hospital, there was at least one other female, Dr. Ruth Saunders. At a staff meeting in October, 1960, when Dr. Leland E. Payton was re-elected president, Dr. Jane T. Carswell was selected to serve as secretary.

Jane wrote home to her mother in a letter dated November 13, 1960:

Here it is after ten on Sunday night and I'm just getting around to the first thing on my list of things to do this week-end. I went over to the Hamman's last night for supper and left at ten pm and then went to the hospital to deliver a baby. This afternoon Ruth (the radiologist) and I went walking in the woods up one of the "hollows" to look for plants. We found a lot of laurel and rhododendron in addition to holly and ferns. White pines grow naturally in the woods around here.

Her love of the outdoors turned to exploring through the surrounding Cumberland mountainsides on her days away from the hospital. She hiked the Kentucky creeks and ridges. She frequented Raven's Rock, a favorite spot for families. Lynch itself had the distinction of being the Kentucky's highest town, and nearby, full of hiking opportunities, was the state's highest point, Black Mountain.

She made a life for herself…until one day when she received a notice. All personnel of the hospital received the same May 27, 1961 letter. "Notre Dame Hospital will discontinue services on July 1, 1961." A thank you letter for her "loyal and efficient" service was included.

The official notice confirmed an article in the May 18 edition of the *Tri-City News* reporting the potential closing. Financial problems resulting from lay-offs in the mines had decreased the number of paying patients. Notre Dame Hospital would be converted to a clinic with no overnight patients. There was no plan, nor money, for Dr. Jane Triplett Carswell to be included. After only one year, she would soon be without a job.

She began a search, using the same essential criteria as before, small town, and was disappointed when she discovered nothing available near her family. One day she piled into a car with three other women in her same job-seeking situation, all in a medical field, and headed to interviews in Hickory, North Carolina. They drove from Kentucky, down the cliffs of the Blue Ridge Mountains to the foothills until they arrived at a huge traffic circle at the major intersection known by the locals as Smith Crossroads. They were not all that far from their Hickory destination when they diverted away from the circle for a quick trip through the small village of Lenoir, North Carolina. She had heard there was an opening in a hospital there.

It was a possibility to investigate.

6

The Practice

"Family medicine keeps one humble. Often you as a physician can do very little to help the patients, but they still give you their trust and share their joys and sorrows with you."
Jane Carswell, *Family Practice Hi-Lights*,
Medical College of Virginia Student Family Practice Association
Winter, 1984

 Lenoir, North Carolina in the early sixties boasted of a population slightly over ten thousand, small enough to interest Dr. Jane Carswell and perhaps, she hoped, large enough to support one more physician. With textile and furniture industries hiring workers, a potential for economic growth was in place. The Lenoir Cotton Mill and its Blue Bell Plant produced increasingly popular jeans for the many new styles coming onto the market in the sixties. Other textile plants dotting the county turned out socks and shirts and a wide variety of knitted cloth.

More than textiles however, with the surrounding tree-covered mountains promising an ample supply of wood, Lenoir became noted for the production of fine furniture. Several family owned businesses sprang up through the years, among them Fairfield Chair, Hammary, Kincaid, Bernhardt and Broyhill.

Arriving in Lenoir a generation earlier than Jane was a surgeon, Dr. Verne Blackwelder. He married Lillie Broyhill, a daughter of one of the Broyhill founders, and soon saw the need for a quality hospital that would offer the best up-to-date equipment and surgical procedures. In 1931 he opened a ten-bed clinic on the second floor over a bank in Lenoir, then in 1934, built a sixteen-bed facility, Blackwelder Hospital near his original clinic. Next door to the hospital was a large apartment facility built specifically to house the nurses.

Blackwelder Hospital soon developed a reputation as an excellent, well run institution providing the best of care with frequently updated equipment. The telemetry unit there had the first monitoring device in the county for cardiac disease. Their patient rooms were considered luxurious and inviting. As an added extravagance, included in the patient's room with no extra charge were pillows equipped with a radio system for listening enjoyment. Some patients begged to stay longer. Dr. Blackwelder took pride in every aspect of the hospital, making sure the floors were clean and polished to a spit shine, and that the kitchen had the best food in town. The cafeteria became a gathering place on Sundays after church when groups from all faiths often stopped in following morning worship and joined with Dr. Blackwelder for the best southern fried chicken in Lenoir.

By the time Jane drove past the front of the building on her job-finding tour, the hospital had increased in size beyond forty beds. There were X-ray machines, laboratory capabilities, a maternity ward and a nursery. Surgical rooms held the newest equipment money could buy. In the basement of the hospital was a pharmacy and rooms for private practice. One was available.

Jane got it.

Notre Dame Hospital in Kentucky closed on June 30, 1961. Her first day on the job at Lenoir's Blackwelder Hospital was August 1, 1961. Between those dates she moved into a small upstairs (non-

From the top, Doris Slayton, Jane, and Nancy Gwyn

airconditioned) two room apartment next door to the first friend she made in her new town, Nancy Carson [Gwyn]. Through her, Jane met a second friend, Wini Harding, who worked in the hospital at the laboratory, and another friend, Doris Slayton. Jane soon was on her way to creating a life of her own.

Jane described her first days living in Lenoir to her brother, John and his wife, Betty, in a letter dated August 2, 1961:

This is my second day at "work" and I'm mostly just sitting here looking at the walls and catching up on my correspondence...My office hours are until 5 every day except Wednesday, and on Thursday, until 9 pm. I'll have to work only one Sunday a month...My first patient was a nice old lady, 84 years old. We had a good time talking about how she used to plow with oxen up in the mountains. She had a daughter who froze to death in a snowstorm near Boone two years ago.

What Jane didn't mention to her brother was that she was not the first female doctor in Lenoir. She would not have to face the obstacle of breaking new ground since three women doctors had paved the way ahead of her and had not allowed gender to interfere with serving the community. In her book, *A Medical History of Caldwell County*, local historian Nancy Alexander wrote about Dr. Margaret Jones Sturgis who joined her physician husband in Lenoir in 1916 but left a year later when he enlisted in the service during World War I. During her short tenure, she introduced the concept of prenatal care to the county and was the first physician to encourage hospital deliveries. However, the only hospital in town, Foothills Sanitorium closed after their departure, although it reopened in 1926 as Caldwell Hospital.

She was replaced in 1917 by Dr. Caroline McNairy, a former school teacher in the county who was from a medical family. Her father was a doctor. Her brother Dr. Banks McNairy had practiced medicine in Lenoir before moving to Kinston, North Carolina. Another of her brothers, John, was a pharmacist and operated the McNairy Drug Store in town. Her nephew was Dr. Verne Blackwelder. Although her practice covered all aspects of medicine, Dr. McNairy became known as the baby doctor at Blackwelder Hospital.

The other female doctor preceding Jane, Dr. Marjorie Strawn, quickly earned the respect of the community after she arrived in Lenoir in the fifties. Like Dr. McNairy, she loved delivering babies and grew a wide practice with children and adults. After years in private practice, she became the county Medical Health Director. During her tenure, the health department made remarkable progress, especially in the rural areas of the county that had little access to medical care.

With Dr. McNairy nearing the end of her career and Dr. Strawn still in the process of establishing her own career, Jane found ready-made supporters to mentor her through her adjustments to Lenoir. Most of all, they were devout Christians who, like Jane intended to do, lived out their faith as they practiced their medicine.

In March of 1964, Dr. Charles Scheil moved his practice from western Virginia (not all that far across the mountain ridges from Lynch, Kentucky) to Blackwelder Hospital. Dr. Scheil reports that he and Dr. Carswell had similar practice desires and soon developed a professional relationship that worked well for many decades. They had a similar philosophy on how to treat patients approaching them with a "How can I help you? What brought you here?" attitude that narrowed to the problem of their immediate concern. Their waiting rooms were often crowded since they each devoted as much time as necessary to an individual dealing with an illness or injury, regardless of how backed up the line became.

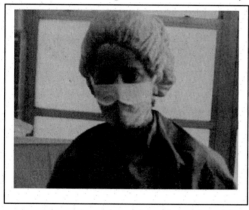

Both of them practiced medicine independent of the other, even though they covered each other's patients when necessary and shared call along with other doctors in evenings and on weekends. They valued each other's opinions when making decisions for patient care, and although they did not always follow the same path of treatment for their patients, they developed a trust and respect in talking through issues.

They also shared expenses, with both doctors employing personnel in an attempt to maintain comradery in the office. Nurses worked mainly with one particular doctor, but they were assigned to both when needed. Dr. Scheil and Dr. Carswell did not share income, however. What Jane earned was hers. What he earned was his. That system allowed them to offer services free of charge on occasion, which Jane did as a response to her faith and to her memories as a child growing up poor. Neither doctor charged a fee to a minister, yet by this system, any income lost did not come out of the other's pocket. They simply marked "NC" on the form, "No Charge." A new office worker once remarked, "If they'd quit sending back people from North Carolina, we could pay the bills here!" No one was turned away.

Family practitioners focused on preventative as well as curative medicine, feeling the relationship with people was a key element of providing care. Jane made rounds in the hospitals. She assisted with surgeries. She met her patients at the emergency room door when they called for help.

Although off duty she was fun-loving and often expressed her tremendous sense of humor in a little chortle of laughter, her demeanor changed the moment she needed to be the serious-minded physician. Her patients were not just chart numbers in the files. They were people with life stories that needed to be treated with dignity and respect. She worked hard and she expected those around her to work hard as well. As a result, she was strict and meticulous. She was kind and gentle, but firm when dealing with important issues. She was soft spoken, but very direct and forceful in what she said in her quiet voice. She was small in stature at five foot three and barely above a hundred pounds, but large in unyielding strength when necessary to advocate for her patients. She was the kind of doctor that could empty bedpans in the morning and attend the opera at night. She was passionate in everything she did, whether dealing with a nurse, participating in church ministries or growing beautiful roses to deliver to unsuspecting friends. She knew of her nurses' art council displays or published poems and made a point to congratulate them. She would not waste a minute of her time. If she found ten extra minutes, she filled it by writing.

She relished the family relationship side of being a physician. She was invited to patients' birthday parties, graduations, and weddings. She received cards from them, thank you notes and Christmas wishes. In turn she sent congratulations when newspaper articles announced their awards or accomplishments. Susan Cogdell Schilling offers an example of Dr. Carswell's relationship with her patients:

Doctor Carswell was friendly and knowledgeable. She seemed to always know what was wrong, and how to fix it. As a child I was baffled that she figured out my ear ache was caused by a piece of playdough lodged in my ear canal...Doctor Carswell was more than just a doctor. She exemplified what a home town doctor should be. She was not only interested in our health, but our personal lives as well. I was thrilled to receive a wedding present and card from her on my special day. This small token reminded me that she really cared.

Susan's mother, Mary Caroline Cogdell, added a comparison between medicine in the early years Dr. Carswell practiced and those from later:

She would send you to a specialist, if need be, but most things she took care of at the time of the appointment. One day I was in her office for some problem. I happened to show her what I thought was a pimple that was sore and would not go away. She pulled down her crooked-neck light, looked at it closely and informed me that she did not like the looks of it and wanted to remove it right then. When the report came back, it was cancer, but nothing else needed to be done. She had cut deep enough to get it all. I have had the same thing happen again, but I was sent to a dermatologist, which took weeks for the appointment. He then took a biopsy, sent it off, and then when it came back as cancer, I was sent to a surgeon several weeks later. He then removed it, the same kind of cancer and no bigger than what she removed. Times have changed!!!

Following the family physician concept, Dr. Carswell dealt with as many situations as she could without referring patients to specialists. Once a man came to the office after severely cutting his arm with a chainsaw. Rather than sending him to the emergency room or to a surgeon, Jane spent hours stitching the wounds herself. If a patient arrived with a broken bone, she put a plaster cast on it. Her patients learned to bide their time in the waiting room when she was called away to deliver a baby during her office hours.

Jane enjoyed seeing her patients out in the community, at the grocery stores, at musical events or at church, yet she often cancelled her own personal plans to hurry to the hospital and deliver babies or deal with emergencies. On the other hand, because people felt like she was family, which is what she asked from them, they began to call her for minor emergencies, often in the middle of the night. Eventually she hired an answering service to screen her calls. Baby delivery, the call went through. Often she felt the need to apologize to friends for her answering service when calls from them were screened as well.

Jane's love of the outdoors brought her to cross country skiing, a sport that ultimately became a necessity in times of winter weather when she skied to the hospital from her home to deliver a baby. In the midst of an ice storm another year, she was unable to drive her car uphill into the hospital parking lot. She took off her slippery shoes and walked the remaining distance in her stocking feet. Once when a neighbor's dog was hit by a car, Jane came speeding down the hill on her bicycle, thinking a child had been hurt.

When a dietician at Caldwell Memorial Hospital approached Jane in 1979 about a personal friend in her third year of medical school at the University of Pennsylvania seeking a one-month rotation, Jane did not hesitate to offer help. This student, Rita Redberg, was searching for a learning experience beyond a city setting. Small town Lenoir, with its rural surroundings and southern culture would give this New York City Jewish native a different viewpoint from her norm.

"Stay with me," Dr. Carswell insisted. By that time, she had bought a home not all that far from her original apartment. The inside she stuffed with hand-quilted spreads, crocheted doilies, art work exchanged "in kind" with local artists, and many other generous gifts from her patients. The front and back yards Jane lined with rose bushes and flower beds. Rita appeared at the door with a bottle of wine as a hostess gift, not realizing this was a "teetotaler" she was moving in with. Jane graciously accepted the gift and added it to the many other unopened bottles of wine in her gift collection under the kitchen sink. The two began a friendship that continued as Rita went on to have a distinguished career as a cardiologist.

Dr. Scheil became aware of a program sponsored by Duke University in Durham, North Carolina where he had attended medical school. Duke sent an invitation to select graduates to bring future physicians into their communities, nurture them, and introduce them to the reality of a medical practice. Because they essentially worked as a team, Dr. Carswell also agreed to become a part of the program. Students shadowed them in the first days after arriving, and then began to see the patients on their own with either doctor following behind them to insure patient care was to their standards. All this demanded extra paperwork and essential time, but they both felt it was a service to Duke University and the medical community. Officially Jane's title was Clinical Assistant Professor of Community Medicine and Family Practice. Unofficially, she was mentor.

In 1994 she received the Duke University Davison Club's Excellence in Teaching Award. A scholarship in her name was awarded to one of their medical students.

Students arrived in Lenoir for a four week eye-opening experience. Jane convinced her friend Wini Harding to house them, and through the years, a wide variety of personalities and talents found their way to her front door.

Dr. Scott Lurie was one of them. As a medical student, he, like many others, roomed with Wini and followed Jane through her day. Years later he wrote a thank you letter to Jane enclosing an article his mother found about her in *Vogue Magazine*. He laughed and teased that her fame had spread "all the way to the fashion circles of New York." He continued:

I learned the important fundamentals of medicine in Lenoir. There is no question that I learned more facts at Duke, but in Lenoir, I learned the beginnings of confidence and a proper attitude to medicine. At Duke there is so much emphasis placed on being exactly right and knowing obscurities in such an involved system of channels and hierarchies, that the medical student is often lost. As a student you get very little responsibility and when you are unsure of yourself, it is difficult to try to wrest that responsibility from the higher ups...Working in your office I did not find that to be the case. I felt that I had quite a bit of freedom and responsibility. I had the freedom of knowing that you would check the findings and that mistakes were not occasion for humiliation, but were occasion for teaching.

Equally as important, I had the responsibility of writing the orders and prescriptions and discussing prognosis, treatment and follow-up with patients. As minor a thing as it might sound to someone who has been in practice for a few years, all of those were anxiety invoking for me. Knowing just enough medicine to know that there are a myriad of conflictions to the various medications used and not enough to know how to sort them out, it was at first difficult to write [prescriptions] for penicillin (What happens if they have an allergic reaction?) ...I learned to trust the PDR and my own judgment and to be comfortable asking questions...I wanted to thank you for making those learning opportunities available to me, tell you what a superb teacher I think you are, and encourage you to continue taking Duke students. Besides Ms. Harding would have to do without the company if you stopped.

A few long blocks away from Jane's home was Caldwell Memorial Hospital, a small county facility that had opened in 1951 and was named as a memorial to honor county servicemen and women of all wars. The original Caldwell Hospital facility closed and later reopened as Hilltop Rest Home. A second privately owned hospital in Lenoir, the Dula Hospital that had opened in 1935 under the leadership of Dr. Fred Dula, at this time converted to a clinic. Blackwelder Hospital, however, remained open for several additional years, shrinking to a twenty-five bed facility in the main section of the building to create more office space for additional physicians. After the death of Dr. Blackwelder, the driving force behind the hospital, it slowly decreased in the population it served. By the late seventies, only Drs. Carswell and Scheil were hospitalizing their patients at Blackwelder.

In 1981 a group of investors built Mulberry Medical Park, a facility adjacent to the county hospital with rooms to house several physician practices. Dr. Carswell and Dr. Scheil selected rooms on the second floor, hers in the corner because she liked the view of the mountains from her office window. Jane filled their waiting room with a menagerie of toy animals (the favorite, a four-foot tall wooden giraffe designed by her sister, Madeline, and built by her father and brother, John), small tables, books and miniature chairs for children. In her own office she placed the roll top desk that once belonged to her father, Rev. Carswell.

The first year Jane moved to the medical park, as a joke on her birthday, her nursing staff brought something she "missed" from being in her previous location. Conveniently located across the road from the entrance lobby to her previous office was Smithey's Department Store with its favorite lunch counter offering, a thick, juicy hamburger and greasy fries. Patients often stopped in the store, picked up an order and brought it with them to eat in the waiting room before their appointments. Jane complained frequently about the greasy smell drifting into her office. Although this simple gift of a Smithey's hamburger and fries brought a smile to her face in her new office, she chose not to eat. She took it home with her, but she admitted the next day that it was quite delicious after all.

Running the business side of a medical practice continued to make demands of Jane's time. She much preferred the humanitarian side of being a physician, yet she often had business decisions to make. Although she had kept her rates consistent with Dr. Scheil and other doctors at Blackwelder, she found at times to be more controlled by outside elements. In the early eighties, President Richard Nixon froze the medical charges for reimbursement of Medicare visits at eleven dollars. Patients would have to pay out-of-pocket any differences they charged. When new doctors coming in were permitted to charge twenty-three dollars a visit, Drs. Carswell and Scheil stopped accepting Medicare for a short period of time. During the Reagan administration in the mid-eighties, every doctor was declared equal, and when fees increased to fifteen dollars a visit, they again began to accept Medicare patients. In another situation that temporarily affected Jane's practice, the government once withheld reimbursements for two months in order to have available money to operate.

Attracting new doctors to small town Lenoir proved to be a constant challenge for the medical community. A North Carolina state agency, the Office of Rural Health, helped place family doctors into small underserved towns. Through this program, in September of 1982, Dr. Nancy Morgan joined with those at Blackwelder Hospital, taking a temporary upstairs office. She was promised a place in the new medical park facility, but its construction was behind schedule. Instead, fresh out of residency at a state-of-the-art university, she stepped into a building from the thirties with uneven, creaky wooden floors and old-fashioned luxuries that were no longer appropriate.

Being women in a predominately male occupation brought the two doctors together in a common bond, and Jane soon became her mentor as she transitioned from academics to reality. Although Dr. Morgan's background prepared her to be an effective doctor, Jane walked her through being an effective Caldwell County doctor. To introduce her to a support community and to make her feel more at home during her first days in Lenoir, Jane held a small afternoon gathering of local business and professional women at her home.

When Dr. Morgan had gone through training, she was told family doctors typically delivered two or three babies a month, but she found a different actuality in Caldwell County. Mothers who were not women of money went to the county health department for their early obstetric care until their eighth month of pregnancy. Then the health department randomly assigned them to family doctors and obstetricians in the area. Added to that, not only did Dr. Carswell have the same rotation of cases from the health department as other physicians like Dr. Morgan, she also had a large following of potential mothers from having practiced in Lenoir for so many years. Although delivering babies was her delight, it was also difficult and exhausting. Jane often delivered babies in an all-night process before going into the office the next day to her scheduled appointments.

Jane saw the need for an improved birthing facility at Caldwell Memorial Hospital, one where mothers could have their babies with

them sooner, and where fathers were included. Traditionally fathers had not been a part of the delivery, but attitudes were changing, and fathers began to demand to be present for the entire delivery. Jane remembered the walls at Dr. McNairy's office coated with hundreds of photographs of babies she had delivered, and she wanted to honor that in some way. She called a local writer and friend from church, Lucy McCarl, to ask a favor. Since Dr. McNairy had delivered Lucy, and then a

generation later had also delivered Lucy's daughter, Jane felt she was the perfect choice for the task. Jane explained her vision, to create a center in the hospital in honor of Dr. McNairy. Would Lucy please write a series of columns for the newspaper about Dr. McNairy and her career delivering babies? That would generate interest in the birthing room and bring in donations. The room was also funded by sales of numerous items Jane made and sold at craft fairs with friend Wini Harding.

Jane held out as long as she could being a cradle-to-the-grave doctor, but she eventually stopped delivering babies when the malpractice insurance rose beyond what could be financially viable. With the comparatively small amount she charged, she could no longer afford the insurance without increasing fees. However, a direct result of her decision to end deliveries was a drop in the number of her pediatric patients. In the past, mothers returned with their children to her family practice, bonding with her as the family doctor who had delivered the baby. That connection no longer existed.

Dr. Scheil became board certified in family practice in 1965, and Jane the year after in 1966. They were the second and third physicians in the county to be board certified in any practice, following Dr. Fred

Thompson in internal medicine. In 1983 Dr. Scheil nominated Jane for an award through the North Carolina Chapter of the American Academy of Family Physicians, and she was recognized as the state Family Physician of the Year. Dr. Scheil surprised her by introducing her at the academy's conference in Greensboro, North Carolina. He talked about working with her on a daily basis. She replied wondering who was watching the shop!

Because of that award, her name went on to the national selection level. The following year she became the first woman to win the American Academy of Family Physicians' National Family Physician of the Year, recognizing that she "defined the true family physician in that she not only saw patients in the office, but attended to patients in the hospital, made house calls, delivered babies, and assisted in surgeries, all while being involved in bettering the community around her." She was selected by a distinguished panel of judges: Dr. Timothy Johnson, medical reporter for ABC's "Good Morning America" show; Ms. Jane Chestnut, Health Editor, Woman's Day magazine; Senator Paula Hawkins (R-Fla); Dr. Bernard Fogel, Dean, University of Miami School of Medicine; and Mrs. Harold Davis, national chairman of volunteers, National American Red Cross Headquarters.

She received a letter of congratulations from Roger Tusken, executive vice president of the American Academy of Family Physicians, Kansas City, Missouri inviting her to participate in the opening ceremony of the 1984 Scientific Assembly by being seated on the platform. For weeks after she was first aware of the award, she was groomed to become a celebrity. In all her medical and humanitarian work, Jane had been consistently behind the scenes. She wanted to make things happen, but did not seek credit. She wanted results. Now, however she was front and center stage, and as uncomfortable as she might have felt, she accepted the attention, describing it as, "more unbelievable than anything else." She did not get caught up in the excitement of national recognition, however, but took the limelight in stride as a part of the duties of representing her profession. She accepted much of the attention because the award showcased the family physician concept and the causes she embraced. She was handed a press packet with advice on dealing with controversial questions reporters might ask, and reminded that she was not speaking for the organization, but for herself. In late August, a camera crew from NBC shadowed her as she went about her day seeing patients and visiting the two projects she was noted for, the shelter home for battered and abused women, and a biracial community.

The award was to be announced the morning of October 8, 1984 on NBC's Today Show. She flew to New York City and prepared to be interviewed by host, Jane Pauley. "I was nervous. They put a dab of make-up on me in five minutes and ran a comb through my hair." With the majority of the segment prerecorded in Lenoir weeks before, the actual live portion amounted to around three minutes. "It was all over before I realized it," she told a *Hickory* (North Carolina) *Daily Record* reporter.

She then flew to Kansas City to accept the award, represented by a small statue of Asclepius, the Greek god of medicine, which she put on display in her office. Interviews with her by an AP correspondent and by UPI Health Editor Patricia McCormack spread over the wires, and their articles about her appeared nationwide. She was in magazines. She was on the radio. If she became discouraged and wanted the turmoil to end, she only had to read letters of encouragement like the one from an admirer in Texas, "Please allow the press to write about you. It can only help the status of women in medicine and perhaps encourage the rest of us to become involved in community life." Jane was later interviewed by a reporter from *Family Weekly*, an insert supplement in newspapers throughout the nation, and the flurry of responses began again. She heard from people looking for help with their medical situations, from a couple wanting to adopt, and from organizations planning shelters for abused and battered women. One friend sent her a clipping from a Mexico City newspaper, and another clipping came from London. She received letters from physicians she had gone to school with or practiced with, or in many cases, from ones she had never met, but felt a kinship to her. The University of North Carolina at Chapel Hill awarded her the Distinguished Alumnus Award on University Day, October 12, 1985 in recognition of her "outstanding contributions to humankind." She was one of five people chosen by the faculty and trustees to receive the award that year.

She was the guest of North Carolina Governor Jim Hunt at the executive mansion in Raleigh. President Ronald Reagan congratulated her with the message,

Your career in medicine enhances the image of the family doctor and your understanding of the close relationship between health and the problems of daily life have led you to even wider service to your community. It is difficult to decide which of your activities is the most noteworthy...Your life is an inspiration not just to your community but to the nation. It is a privilege to send my congratulations and gratitude to you.

The Lenoir Rotary Club endowed an annual scholarship in her honor to be awarded to a nursing student at Caldwell Community College and Technical Institute. The Omicron Chapter of Alpha Delta Kappa, an organization for outstanding women educators, sponsored her for their state level Distinguished Woman Award. Jane was guest lecturer at the University of North Carolina, at East Carolina University, at East Tennessee State University, as well as at the medical school she had once attended in Virginia. The fame of being the National Family Physician for 1984-85 soon became a part of her past. The cameras turned off, the reporters stopped calling, and she went back to her real passions, providing medical care to her patients and responding to humanitarian needs. She appreciated all the well wishes, saying only, "The award business has been very interesting."

Lenoir News-Topic, Photo by David Freeman

Caldwell County Commissioners read a declaration they had prepared in her honor.

As part of maintaining her license to practice medicine she attended conferences throughout the world and often had fellow doctors comment about her award, but that, too, faded. She was a member of a local professional organization, the Caldwell County Medical Society, where physicians met monthly as a community for not only professional reasons, but also for socializing. Here she was on equal ground as she exchanged stories and expressed concern with others about the direction the practice of medicine was heading, becoming increasingly technical and highly gadget oriented. In 1999 she and Charles Hooper with Caldwell Memorial Hospital's Environmental Services tied in votes for the Employee of the Year Award. Both had been Employee of the Month earlier that year. Their prize was either a three day trip to the beach or five hundred dollars. Both of them chose the money, but Jane requested that her share be given to Charles.

By the time Dr. John McMenemy arrived in Lenoir in the mid-nineties, Dr. Carswell and Dr. Scheil had sold their practices to the hospital. This change removed the business aspect of medicine from their shoulders and allowed them to concentrate more on what they were most passionate about, providing care to their patients. Each of them was beginning to consider retirement in the not so distant future and were planning accordingly. They renovated an area on their floor in Mulberry Medical Park to add extra examining rooms and an office for Dr. McMenemy. One final time, the two successfully brought a fresh-from-residency physician out of the textbook and into the reality of practicing medicine in Lenoir, North Carolina. Dr. McMenemy tapped into their vast experiences, finding both of them, he says, to be approachable with any medical questions he came across. From them he developed the ability to hand examine a patient, a skill slowly dying because of the prevalence of modern ultrasounds and various blood tests. They taught him clues they watched for as they checked a neck or abdomen, or when they listened to a heart. They taught him how they observed a patient walk into the room. They taught him what their experiences had taught them. They knew their patients would be in good hands, because they had trained those hands. And so they retired.

Dr. Scheil left first, in 1998.

Dr. Jane Triplett Carswell, in 1999.

Photograph by Spencer Ainsley, courtesy of Lenoir News-Topic

The treasured roll top desk in her
office once belonged to her
father, Rev. Arthur Carswell.
After her death it was kept by her
brother John's family.

Part II

HUMANITARIAN

7

Interracial Relations

"Protecting the dignity of people is what that was all about."
Jane Carswell, *The Modesto* (California) *Bee*
October 28, 1984

When Jane Carswell arrived in Lenoir in 1961, she knew nobody, except perhaps the principal at Lenoir High School, Henry McFayden, and even then only by a thin thread of a connection. He was a nephew of the medical missionary who inspired her to become a doctor in the first place. She did have distant relatives in the South Mountains of the adjoining county, but none that she knew personally. She also had worked with a nurse, Suggie Styres, at Rex Hospital in Raleigh who coincidentally also found her way to Lenoir. And yet, if she were going to make a life for herself, Jane realized she would have to create it from scratch.

She turned to that one important part of her life, the church, looking no further than First Presbyterian Church. There she found what she was searching for, not only nurturing inspiration to strengthen her faith, but also a "family" made up of members who cared for each other as they cared for the world around them. Because this church facility was located in the center of town, members considered part of their faith purpose was to look into the community in which they were immersed, see the needs, and take action.

Over the years she became a part of First Church's Sojourners Sunday School Class, and as the name indicates, started on a faith journey with them that challenged her to discover the meaning of being

Christian and following her faith and her heart. They studied together, discussing freely with no question discouraged, and no doubts ignored. Jane believed God expected her to go beyond her personal boundaries. Living out her faith was a part of her belief system. She strengthened her resolve not to get caught up in settling for whatever society dictated.

She was selected in 1971 by First Presbyterian Church as their first woman ruling elder (the church's governing body) when the position became open to both genders. Her minister father approved. Her mother was thrilled, knowing her daughter was not afraid to speak her mind despite being female and small in stature, and that her faith was bigger than her body.

This faith in action was tested time and again, but not so much as during the racial tensions sweeping across the south in the sixties and early seventies. Growing up in the segregated south, Jane knew society's expectations. While she attended the whites-only school, the black children she played with at home attended their separate school on the other side of town. Her mother brought in children of all races for summer Bible School and taught that the God she believed in was the same God for everyone, yet on Sunday mornings, they worshiped in different churches. During her years at Flora Macdonald, Jane continued her mother's mission and taught Bible in the black schools, and yet, as society dictated, drank from a public water fountain in town labeled "Whites Only."

Her medical school training had been in downtown Richmond, Virginia where she provided care for people of all races. She didn't check for color. She checked for symptoms. She held wrists taking pulses. She felt for lumps on necks. She prodded abdomens. She delivered babies and rejoiced with new mothers, black and white alike.

In 1954 the United States Supreme Court, in the Brown vs Board of Education of Topeka, Kansas had declared the segregated educational facilities that Jane knew as a child to be "inherently unequal." Desegregation of schools in North Carolina was overseen by the Department of Health, Education and Welfare (HEW) and supported by the Fourth Circuit Court of Appeals in Richmond. No changes came to Lenoir until each local school system was required to submit plans for integration in compliance with Title VI of the Civil Rights Act of 1964. Systems not in compliance would lose any federal financial assistance.

Lenoir and Caldwell County operated two school systems at that time, city and county. In the city itself were two high schools, Lenoir High School for white students from inside the city limits with principal, Henry McFayden, and Freedman High School for all black students throughout the county with principal, Montrose L. DeVane. These schools were dearly loved by their respective communities and had firmly established traditions extending back generations. Both city and county systems developed their respective required plans for compliance for the 1965-66 school year, with black students from outside the city limits being assigned to county schools. All high school students from inside the city limits would attend Lenoir High School. Freedman High School would be converted into Lenoir Junior High School.

At times during this transition there were significant expressions in the black community about particular concerns. Since Dr. Carswell's patient load included people from the African American community, often she was the person they could turn to and talk with. The black families needed someone to listen and she had an understanding ear to offer.

There was much fear and suspicion throughout both the black and white communities in town. Rumors made people afraid to enter neighborhoods of different races. Her friend Jennie Deal writes about Jane, "It was not without some fear for the blacks to ride in an area that was traditionally 'white.' All fears were put aside when one was around Jane - it just wasn't part of the equation."

Racial tension increased and came to a head when a group of black students walked out of class one day in February 1971 in response to an incident at a basketball game the previous night. They marched together on the street past Blackwelder Hospital. Jane was the physician for many of these students and their families, both black and white. She could not keep silent, realizing Lenoir was on the verge of the same violence that was burning throughout the south. She felt strongly that she needed to be part of the group that was getting the two races together.

She was determined, and she had no qualms about speaking up even though she found she did not always have everybody patting her on the back as she took a stand against racial injustices. Yet she persevered, and her strong influence helped to diffuse racial tension and further understanding throughout the community.

She made phone calls. She knocked on doors. She invited twelve key people to a meal at her home, asking, "What can we do?" She helped organize the Bi-Racial Fellowship of Concerned Citizens made up of Christians from different faiths and races. The group began meeting and talking and praying together. They developed a faith based interracial council.

They worked diligently that first year, creating opportunities for the two races to interact over meals and events. They went on a retreat to Montreat Conference Center in Black Mountain, North Carolina. They also chaperoned youth retreats to the center where students learned that regardless of who they were or where they came from, they must learn to put themselves in the place of the other person. For many whites who attended, this was their first experience of sitting down and having meaningful discussions with blacks. They had not been raised in bi-racial schools. Neither had Jane, but she was the encourager, expecting those around her to be a part of bringing the community together. About two hundred students and adults once spent the weekends at the center and got to know each other better as they climbed mountains, played, listened to talks, had discussions, roller skated and worshipped together. One Sunday

they attended church services there, and some of the group sat on the same pew as Billy Graham and his family.

The committee sponsored hot dog roasts and back to school parties to bring students together. When the first picnic was held, over two hundred children, both black and white, their parents, and teachers were served hot dogs and hamburgers with all the trimmings. People from both races had donated money for this picnic, and the all-white Lenoir Country Club let them store food in their facilities in preparation. A popular band, the White Heat performed. Eventually the need for many of the activities abated, leaving the one remaining event that became Dr. Jane Carswell's passion, the Annual Bi-Racial Christmas program. For her, "It's what

Christmas is all about. That is why I have to be there." She wrote a dialogue to present at the 2014 program that told the story behind the attempts to develop racial harmony in the community:

HOW IT ALL BEGAN
Interracial Christmas Program, December, 2014

Becky Stevens: We want to tell you a story tonight. It began in a small town in the foothills of North Carolina. Two groups of people lived there but in two distinctly separate areas.

Helen Hall: They hardly mixed at all as I remember—at work, in schools, or churches.

Becky: There was some mixing in the schools and work, but almost never in the churches. At work one group mainly worked for the other.

Helen: That wasn't a good situation.

Becky: You're right. One cold February night in 1971 a fight broke out at a high school basketball game between two people—one from each group. Authorities at the game panicked and called the police.

Helen: Most people thought that that was an overreaction.

Becky: Well, it was. When the police (seven of them) arrived, they arrested the victor in the fight as the other participant had already left.

Helen: Folks were really upset.

Becky: You'd better believe it! The friends of the boy arrested protested, and mace was used to break up the crowd.

Helen: I heard that two of the protestors were arrested and hauled off to jail, too.

Becky: You're right, and it was told that they were beaten there. This set the stage for tension between the two groups at school the next day.

Helen: There were several fights, and even the "sacred" trophy case was broken. School let out early.

Becky: Police met the students who were friends of the ones arrested the night before outside the school and told them to "Hit the street and get to your part of town." And did they ever, in a huge protest march.

Helen: Things began to get violent.

Becky: Really bad. Students shouted obscenities at the police and were hit with night sticks. Rocks were thrown and two policemen were knocked to the ground. Gun shots were fired by the police. Fire trucks were called.

Helen: The junior high school was stormed and a teacher was beaten up in his classroom.

Becky: One brave white man marched with protestors back to their part of town. By now you know that this was a racial problem. This man was Louis Zbinden, pastor of First Presbyterian Church at that time. Louis, Rev. F. D. Battle, and Rev. W. W. Edwards got the crowd in a building by promising to listen to them. Rev. Battle urged them to stop fighting. "Some people will get killed," he said. "They have guns, and you have only rocks." The police chief and city council members were called and came to the meeting. They listened to complaints for several hours.

Helen: Things quieted down a little, but there was no school for two days.

Becky: Tensions were high. Rumors were rampant. People had many complaints—police brutality, lack of representation on important committees and governing bodies, partiality of the judicial system, especially not letting Blacks take out warrants against the police.

Helen: The city Human Relations Board met nineteen times and heard anyone who wished to talk.

Becky: Government bodies, the city council, the school board, and the press all tried to find solutions.

Helen: One reason we have the Interracial Christmas Worship Service yearly is because of one city council member, George Bernhardt, Sr. He observed, "If anyone ought to help solve racial issues, it should be the Christian churches."

Becky: From that statement a small group calling themselves the Bi-racial Group of Concerned Christians gathered and listened to each other as Christian brothers and sisters.

Helen: For over two years around a dozen people gathered every other Sunday night and heard each other's concerns and prayed together. School did start more smoothly, but it's the first Christmas after that I remember most. A small group, about fifteen people, of Concerned Christians decided to have a Christmas meal and worship service together. A covered dish meal was shared, scripture read, carols sung, and Rev. Battle led in prayer.

Becky: The group continued to meet every other week. Different people were there depending on their interests.

Helen: A variety of people were invited, such as school personnel, representatives of the press, government officials, law enforcement personnel, and judges.

Becky: It was an atmosphere in which people could be honest with each other as varied topics came up, such as interracial dating, lack of news of the Black community (except for the bad) in the newspaper, and the fact that Black wedding announcements were not printed. School problems were discussed. The housing problem was a big one. Whites were surprised to learn of Black ghettoes in the county and that Blacks were limited as to where they could live.

Helen: A result of that was Town and Country Housing Development—the first integrated housing in Caldwell County. Rev. Parker Williamson led the drive for this with help from Robert Winchester, Sam Sturgis, Barbara Frieman, Helen Banner, Joan Suddreth, Jim McCarl, Jane Carswell, Rev. W. W. Edwards, Zalia Hemphill, John Christian Bernhardt, Margaret Phillips and others.

Becky: We have had the Christmas worship service for the past forty-three years.

Helen: At first we had a covered dish dinner together followed by the worship service. The people who attended the county's free meals program were invited, and did they ever enjoy the food. After eating all they could they would take a heaping plate home "for a friend."

Becky: One of the most memorable times was the night we ran out of food. Someone on the radio announced that they were serving a free meal at the church to anyone who wanted it—just come and get it. The miracle of the Loaves and Fishes was repeated before our eyes. Alex Bernhardt and George Hancock found enough cash in their pockets and went to Kentucky Fried Chicken and replenished the table—and there was some left over.

Helen: This Christmas service is unique in that there is no sermon and no collection. God's message of "Peace on Earth" and the gift of His Son has been presented in drama, liturgical dance, with puppet productions, by story tellers, monologues, and chalk talks. They have even featured Sam Sturgis and his musical saw.

Becky: One of the main things has been the music. We have worshipped, thanked and praised God with many types of music—praise bands, Gospel choirs, hand bells, children's choirs, instrumentals, and many others. Who will ever forget Margaret Phillips and her beautiful voice? Or the Hispanic band and its toe-tapping version of "Feliz Navidad"?

Helen: Some problems in our community have been solved, but there are still areas of injustice. The one thing we do affirm is that we are all God's children and none of us is perfect. He loves us all and wants us to love and care for each other. He sent His Son to save us all from our sins and gives the promise of life eternal in His kingdom.

Each year continuing through to the Christmas following Jane's death in 2015, the churches in Lenoir came together for this worship celebration. The first few years had included a covered dish supper following the program, but after the crowds increased beyond the logistics, the fellowship element of the evening changed to a reception with light refreshments. Because the facilities at First Presbyterian Church could accommodate large crowds, the event was held there for several years until the location alternated between churches of various denominations and races, at buildings that could seat two or three hundred. Every program included the carol "O, Come All Ye Faithful," and always concluded with, until the year of his death, a benediction by Rev. Venoy Pearson. One year Jane suggested they write blessings on a slip of paper to put in a basket and pass around as a reverse offering, taking blessings out.

Jane's friends knew she would be calling on them for help each October, and they willingly accepted. During the yearly planning sessions, program possibilities were discussed. She called those suggested individuals or groups saying, "I know you have this talent, will you come and perform?" They did.

One meeting night was at the home of Herb and Becky Stevens. After a dinner and the planning session, those attending went to their cars parked in the driveway, only to find the road was flooded from heavy rains. Despite several attempts, no one could get out. The bridge had washed away and in the darkness, no one attempted to leave. They all returned to the Stevens' house and held an overnight pajama party with a thrown-together breakfast the next morning. In the daylight they were able to set planks across the water and meet rides on the opposite side, but their cars remained stranded for several days.

Eventually the name of the event changed from the Bi-Racial Christmas Program to the Interracial Christmas Program, incorporating the third culture in Lenoir, the Latino community. Few Hispanics lived in Caldwell County in 1971 when the programs began, but by the end of the century, they made up thirteen percent of the population. A new yearly tradition began with members of St. Francis Catholic Church singing "Feliz Navidad." The rhythm of the Yax brothers' Preciosa Sangre de Christo added a new dimension of worship beyond the mellow tones of church handbells or the grace of a dance interpretation that had been a part of past years.

The 2001 Christmas program included a short skit presented by Happy Hands Puppets, a ministry that had roots in the medical field. Having a child talk to a puppet was a technique counselors and medical personnel often used when working with young children who were

Happy Hands Puppeteers

afraid. Jane felt adults would respond to puppets as well. The puppet could be a vehicle to break down barriers and to teach the Bible. Along with Mary Alice Norwood, Joan Suddreth and Helen Dixon, she helped create the puppet ministry. Mary Alice and Jane traveled to Woodbridge, Virginia to attend workshop training in puppets. With the help of Ken Roberts, they built a portable stage with PVC pipes. Helen Dixon, a seamstress at Bernhardt Industries, designed the curtains along the front. The Caldwell Arts Council donated funds to purchase puppets. Children from several local churches interacted with each other in rehearsals and at pizza parties. When children had no transportation, Dr. Jane, as they called her, brought them herself. She invited them to her home for cookouts. She wrote songs and scripts that always included a moral lesson featuring lead puppet, and crowd favorite, purple-faced Rufus. First Presbyterian associate pastor, Robert Austell, put several of Jane's lyrics to music. The puppeteers performed often at churches throughout Lenoir.

In the process of meeting with the city's human relations committee, Jane found that one area of great concern to the black community was lack of sufficient housing available to their families. In the Sunday evening conversations within the Bi-Racial Fellowship, the black community pointed out that because of segregation, they lived in certain well-defined areas in the community. As the population grew, those limited areas filled, and families were living with extended family members. Their housing options were constrained by traditional black-white land boundaries, with little opportunities for expansion. With Jane's encouragement, First Presbyterian came to the forefront addressing the housing concern. Under the leadership of then minister, Rev. Parker Williamson, the church created an entity separate and apart from the church, the Caldwell Community Development Corporation. By doing this, they could apply for federal grants without placing the church at financial risk. Church members pledged to undergird the corporation.

Before he arrived in Lenoir in 1970, Rev. Williamson had been involved in the movement for racial justice in other southern states. He had marched with Martin Luther King, Jr. from Selma to Montgomery, Alabama, working on voting rights for African American citizens. As a part of the Lenoir community, he joined with Jane and others in the push to improve the standard of living for all races. This nonprofit corporation the church created raised a substantial amount of money and purchased a hundred fifty acres of property in Dulatown, a small rural community outside the city limits that bordered both black and white family properties.

In the days before Habitat for Humanity organized in the county and furthered the cause for affordable housing, this corporation was there to respond to the need. Town and Country Park, as it was named, was made up of black and white families. Those who qualified purchased a building lot at cost from the corporation. Loans from the Farmers' Home Administration enabled homeowners to borrow enough money to finance an entry level home.

Building these homes became a community effort. Teams of young people helped demolish dilapidated structures on the property. Families came together and worked on building homes for each other. After several homes were completed, a developer expanded the subdivision into a community. In the end, around a hundred homes were built, many for single parents who were finally able to afford a home.

Because of her leadership as chairman of the Lenoir Human Relations Board and her dedication to bettering the community through her service in a variety of on-going projects, she was the "Woman of the Year" recipient of the 1980 Caldwell County Chamber of Commerce's L.A. Dysart Citizenship Award. Presenter Steve Sumlin of the *Lenoir News-Topic*, called her a "mover and a shaker" and described her as one who "shares and cares."

Cleve Reagan, Lenoir News-Topic

Steve Sumlin presenting 1980 L.A. Dysart Woman of Year to Jane Carswell and Man of the Year to Boyd Wilson

Jane often participated in the Martin Luther King, Jr. Day observances organized by the local NAACP by marching through the streets with members of both the black and white communities. The crowd gathered each year at Broyhill Park and marched down Ridge Street to Lenoir's town square. At St. Paul's AME one year, the speaker pointed to Jane and the dozen or so with her from the white community and said, "There are the people who will help you. You can trust them."

He was right.

*The Christmas tree
at her home in Happy Valley*

8

Shelter Home

"He really hit her hard, right in front of me. But she wouldn't press charges. She said she had to go home and live with him, that she didn't have any place else to go."
Jane Carswell, *Charlotte Observer*
December 9, 1984

Being a part of a community allowed Dr. Jane Carswell to witness times of joy, delivering babies that grew up and invited her to a wedding, or curing the sick that sent her heartwarming thank you notes after a long ordeal. But as part of this same community, she also witnessed the misery of life, illnesses that had no resolution other than death, or the aftermath of an action of domestic violence where she patched an arm and sent the victim directly back into the situation. Jane's patients, like patients everywhere, experienced it all, accepting the good and the bad as a part of life.

Except that Jane drew a line. Domestic violence should never be an acceptable part of life. It had gripped too many of her patients by the throat, stomping on their dreams, and keeping them and their children in a state of perpetual anxiety and fear for their lives.

There once was a three inch stab wound. "Bumped into a knife on the kitchen counter," the wife explained as Jane stitched the gash.

There were enough broken bones and bruised eyes that caused Jane to feel she was the medic waiting behind the lines in a battlefront.

Perhaps the single instigating event that finally helped her draw that line happened one defining day after she had delivered a baby. She entered that patient's room for a post-delivery visit. The husband was speaking harshly to his wife, demanding that she get out of the bed, come home immediately, cook his supper, clean the house and tend the other two children as a "real" mother should. Then he hit her...hard...there, in the hospital room, in front of Dr. Carswell. She called authorities, but the mother refused to press charges. She would be going home to him, because she had nowhere else to go.

Dr. Carswell set out to find something for women in that mother's situation, and if she could not find it, she would create it. Jane approached her church asking for help, then the Council on the Status of Women expressing her concerns. A group met around Jane's kitchen table, brainstorming for solutions. They studied possibilities, a shelter perhaps. Their search found one in Atlanta and one in Baltimore, nothing else between, certainly nothing nearby. Jane traveled to Baltimore, interviewed the staff and organizers of the shelter there, and came home with ideas and possibilities.

But first, was there really a need? If so, how could they prove it? After all, spousal abuse was a secret plague, done under cover of closed doors. Their readings found it to be the most unreported crime in America. Would anyone admit to being a victim, much less a perpetrator? For those who claim abuse, would their lives be in jeopardy for bringing the facts out into the open?

In 1977, long before consulting groups began conducting analysis for thirty or forty thousand dollars, a group of determined women in Caldwell County began the process of a needs assessment themselves, using their own methodologies. For two weeks they monitored the emergency room at the hospital and found ten women injured due to abuse. They developed questions for a survey, delving into the hidden corners of domestic violence. They wanted to hear the voice of the people. Is there really a need for a shelter? Do you know someone, or have you yourself experienced this? The local newspaper, the Lenoir News-Topic, announced the survey and the purpose. Committee members spread across the county with their sheets, sending copies home with school students, or leaving others at stores in town, at the furniture and textile plants, or at the laundromats. Mail in your answers, the sheets encouraged, or put them in the boxes placed throughout the community. Members of First Presbyterian helped collect and record the results. Some surveys were returned anonymous, but the majority were signed.

The response was overwhelming. There was a definite need to take immediate action. Based on the findings in the needs analysis, those concerned citizens organized as an advocacy group made up of politicians, professionals and community members, many of whom quietly and anonymously were victims themselves. What they found in the answers people had written was a desperate plea for a safe, if temporary, home for women and children where they could turn in times of domestic trouble, where they could make decisions about the future without fear of reprisal.

Photograph from Shelter Home archives

Original shelter

Next door to the Blackwelder Hospital facility was a two-story apartment house built in the thirties by Verne Blackwelder as housing for nurses at the hospital. It had since been converted to private apartments. This red brick building contained eight bedrooms and bathrooms, two kitchens, and several additional rooms that could be used for meetings or children's play. One rental was open and ready for use. As each lease for the other occupants lapsed, their rooms would also be available. It was the perfect answer for a shelter, not only because of the building itself, but also because of its location around the corner from the Lenoir Police Headquarters.

This core committee developed rules and regulations necessary to establish a successful shelter. There would be a two week limit, flexible if space was available. The clients were to help prepare the meals and share other household duties. They would be screened to weed out those who just needed a place to stay as opposed to those who were truly hurting from abuse. Clients would have a forty-eight hour orientation to learn the rules of the shelter: Do not accept phone calls from the abuser for the first two days. No alcohol or drugs. Women who needed help with substance abuse were referred to other agencies. Foothills Mental Health Center was available for emotional counseling.

The shelter would be charged no rent, and churches in the county offered financial assistance to pay for operating expenses. The Episcopal Diocese of Western North Carolina donated that year's All Saints offering of over five thousand dollars. The Charlotte Diocese of the Catholic Conference donated money, as did many other churches, as well as the Caldwell and Burke chapters of United Way. Jane made phone calls to key individuals in the furniture industry requesting help with furnishing the rooms. With an eight thousand dollar grant, the first executive director was hired, Debi Nelson. Felicite Doll and Doris Robinson with assistant Princess Dula were hired to work with women and children.

A campaign began to draw public attention to the curse of domestic violence and to change society's attitudes. Spousal abuse was a learned behavior, most often from a cycle of abuse experienced in the home as a child. Often the abuser was a victim as well, powerless and growing to adulthood with low self-esteem and believing it was a way of life. Girls from domestic violence typically grew up to marry abusers. This needed to stop. A line had been drawn in Caldwell County.

The shelter opened April 22, 1978. For one week, no one came. Fear kept them away, and wealthy clients felt coming in as a victim would not be socially acceptable. Victims had been beaten down so much, they could not see a resolution, or they had accepted violence as a way of life and could not see a different possibility. When women finally dribbled in, they arrived by themselves or with children in tow, in the middle of the night while the intoxicated husband slept, or in broad daylight while he was away. They did not know when, if ever, they would return home. Debi Nelson remained on site twenty-four hours a day until the shelter eventually hired night house manager, Nan Fender, who received no salary, but lived on the site in exchange for room and board. In the first year, two men sought help from abusive relationships as well, although they were not housed at the shelter.

Clients came without a plan, escaping with only their lives. They had no clothes on their backs, or no toothbrush to claim as their own. Dentists responded with toothbrushes and toothpaste. Civic groups donated major items, like food for the table, and minor items, everyday essentials like laundry detergent.

In those beginning days, the facility in Lenoir was the only shelter for abused women between Baltimore and Atlanta, and the first to open its doors in the state of North Carolina. It charged a fee for those who could afford to pay, a token dollar fifty per day for adults, five dollars for those from outside the county, fifty cents for each child. This sent the message to the women that they were not getting charity, that they were worthwhile. Those from Caldwell County who had no money were sponsored by social services when necessary, and no one was turned away. The shelter gave priority not only to Caldwell County women, but also to those from neighboring Burke County in a "preferred client status" where their commissioners had voted to financially support their citizen's costs. Law enforcement from other counties brought abused women to the shelter because they had nowhere else to turn. Money was available to help out-of-county women travel to courts in their districts so they could testify against their abusers.

Within a year, the scope of the shelter expanded to include victims of sexual assault. The shelter received RASA money from the North Carolina Department of Administration's Council on the Status of Women that enabled them to establish a hotline with the Caldwell Memorial Emergency Room. It became a pilot program with the only twenty-four hour crisis service in the area. A Federal Preventative Health Services block grant helped to train volunteers working with Caldwell Memorial Hospital, area police agencies, the health department, and social services.

In her address at the fortieth anniversary celebration, former Executive Director Debi Nelson told about the volunteers. "We trained them on crisis counseling during initial calls with women over the phone and to listen to them. It was their story and we were there to help...We established several programs to help the women such as counseling, daycare, AA and Al-Anon, job assistance, and clothing exchange."

Governor James B. Hunt awarded the Caldwell County shelter special recognition in 1979. Jane accepted the award in behalf of the shelter. In its initial year and a half of operation, it had served nearly eight hundred clients. However the recession in the eighties forced not just a cutback in services because of lower donations, but also caused an increase in clients because of economic stresses on the families. The shelter remained open through individual donations as well as grants from the Domestic Violence Project and the Council on the Status of Women. A new director was hired, Felicite Doll, who served from 1984 until 1986.

The shelter offered a four-pronged approach to clients through safety, advocacy, recovery and prevention. They took in victims of not only physical violence, but also of mental and verbal abuse. The women often arrived in a state of shock, and rarely were they aware of their legal options. Returning the client to the home was not necessarily considered a failure, but continuing abuse was the outcome to avoid. All cases weren't success stories.

One former resident, a frequent returnee to the shelter home, was killed by her husband. She had finally developed an escape plan and fled out of state, but the husband tracked her down, stalked her and stabbed her.

Another abused wife and client at the shelter served time in prison for stabbing and killing her husband, and in yet another case, one was incarcerated for shooting her husband with a shotgun while he slept. Jane argued each time, "This is wrong. She lived her whole life as a victim of abuse." Jane hurried to the shelter home after each incident because she knew that the caregivers and those delivering services would be impacted by the clients they had worked with.

An official letter arrived in the mail in early 1987 from Blackwelder Properties, the owner of the building. The contract would soon be up for renewal, and they had other plans for the site. The letter was giving them ample notice to vacate within the year. The board must find a new location, preferably near law enforcement and emergency services.

They discussed two possibilities, either finding a replacement house or constructing a new facility. When a one-acre lot downtown became available, they chose the second option. Their plans called for a home with seven resident bedrooms that could accommodate up to twenty-five women and children. Ground breaking for the four thousand, five hundred square foot brick building was held September, 1987. The purchased land also included an older home with three apartments that could be utilized in the future as a transitional step between the emergency shelter and more permanent housing, giving women time to rebuild their lives and learn life skills while overcoming dependency.

Once the location was secured, a fundraising campaign began led by Judy Abee. Dr. Carswell set out to help by making phone calls to corporations and individuals, asking for donations. A trip to London was raffled. Werner Von Trapp, of *Sound of Music* fame, presented free benefit concerts at the Lenoir Mall, with donations accepted at the door.

In early January of 1988, construction at the new site was accelerated because of an unfortunate fire on the second floor of the McNairy building that caused extensive damage. Residents at the shelter had to be evacuated to St. James Episcopal Church while the firefighters extinguished the fire, but the bedrooms were destroyed. All linens were lost and all furnishings burned beyond recovery. The next morning, nearby Smithey's Department Store donated clothes for those residents who had gone through the fire. While the downstairs rooms at the shelter could still be used for office space, the resident shelter was out of commission and clients were sent to other counties for shelter. Once again Jane began calling for help from the community. She turned to the furniture companies for new beds and couches and tables. She phoned churches and hospital employees and friends, and friends of friends to ask for towels and bed linens and anything that could make the new house less institutional. Several foundations in the community donated money for operating expenses.

Photograph from Shelter Home archives
The 1988 Shelter Home

At the grand opening in April of 1988 Rev. Parker Williamson, the keynote speaker, stated that the "public has the responsibility to see that abused and battered women find refuge." In opening this facility, Caldwell County claimed another first in the state of North Carolina, the first building designed and built specifically to be a shelter for abused women. It also claimed that it was totally financed before the first client walked through the doors.

Executive Director, Georgie Stone conducted tours through the private resident area to show to donors how their money had been spent, and then for security and confidentiality reasons, the shelter closed forever to the general public.

This security was tested and revised one morning in March, 1989 during an incident that showed how vulnerable the shelter actually was in the face of a determined abuser looking for his wife. This man planned his attack. First he went to the private home of a worker and, armed with a rifle and taking her four year old child as hostage insurance, forced her to smuggle him through security at the shelter home front door. Once inside, he fired numerous rounds of ammunition. When he did not find his wife, he took hostages and demanded that the police bring her to him. Instead, they surrounded the home and brought in hostage negotiators who talked by phone asking him to release the seven people in the shelter without harming them. During this thirteen-hour standoff they located his wife, who assisted in deescalating the situation. Ultimately no one was hurt, and many lessons were learned about safety and security.

The staff immediately added more lights and "No Trespassing" signs. Over the years, for added protection, the site was surrounded by an eight foot fence that featured an electric gate, a call box, and several cameras watching over the entrance. Women seeking shelter entered through the police station, the hospital, Jane's office in a few cases, or through established safe havens in the county where they went in the front door and disappeared out the back.

The shelter also had to reestablish trust in the community, because the need was still a reality. Statistics from 1991 showed two hundred forty-one crisis calls, one hundred thirty walk-ins, and ninety-nine women assisted in court. One hundred seventy-four children and a hundred forty-five women were provided overnight refuge. A second structure was added for clients who needed long term housing and the original transition house on the shelter property was removed in a controlled burning. This second stage program followed crisis care and clients qualified for federally funded subsidized assistance. Additional capital renovations increased the size of the shelter's area, adding a second floor, and finally patching over the bullet holes in the ceiling tiles that were constant reminders of when things go wrong.

Despite the many precautions, unfortunate incidents still happened to the clients they worked with. One was killed as she returned home to retrieve her clothing. Dr. Carswell had treated this girl when she was a young teenager. She witnessed the abuser come into the medical practice with her several times and sit in the lobby to wait. The Monday after this girl died, Jane came to the shelter, sat down and had a good cry with the arresting officer.

The remodeled shelter,
also known as the Jane Carswell House

Not only did Jane provide medical care to the residents, she provided emotional support to the staff and volunteers. Jane often arrived unexpectedly at any hour with a load of food left over from a dinner or a reception at the church. She cared about the night and weekend workers as much as the regular day staff, wanting all of them to feel a part of the team. She kept a fresh supply of flowers from her yard in the front entrance. In a household of women and children, she also was the toilet paper provider, making sure the shelter never ran out of toilet paper!

CD *image courtesy of John Craig*

A group of musicians from the county donated their time and talents to record Christmas songs as a fund raiser for the shelter home. The picture on the cover was taken by Jane Carswell.

Bell Atlantic Mobile donated wireless cell phones to victims, recognizing the tool as a lifeline for women when they were isolated. Smart Start and the Environmental Enhancement Project provided funds for playground equipment to create a stress-relief play center for the children. Child care volunteers babysat while mothers attended support groups. Other volunteers were trained through the rape crisis program to accompany victims of sexual assault to the hospital or police station. Educational programs on sexual abuse and violence became a part of the Caldwell County school curriculum: "Good Touch/Bad Touch" programs for the youngest, "Conflict Resolution" for the middle grades, and "Dating Violence" for the high schools. There was a men's march against domestic violence through the "Men Holding Other Men Accountable" initiative. There were candlelight vigils. There were posters with catchy slogans, all efforts to change the culture of violence in the home.

The board, along with then executive director Sarah Lowe, campaigned for recognition and community support, emphasizing the goal to eliminate domestic violence within two generations. A series of dedicated executive directors followed her, Pat Carroll, Denise Walker, Terri Looper, Tracey Triplett and Deborah Teeters. Jane was on the board for many of the years, always the quiet member until something needed to be said, when she became vocal, and specific. She encouraged the executive directors, always making sure they realized the significance of their position.

To keep the home in the public consciousness, supporters often sponsored fundraising booths at town events. Once they sold toy ducks Jane had helped make from foam rubber donated by a friend who worked in a furniture plant. One year they made bean bags, and shortly after they sold them, people complained they found weevils crawling from them. Another year they designed and sold frog-shaped doorstops. For several years Jane supplied potted plants she had dug from her own and her friends' gardens for the annual Auction and Plant Sale.

Jane and Ken Roberts working the plant sale

In 2009 Sharon Poarch, one of the hostage negotiators from the earlier incident, was hired as executive director. By that time she had retired after thirty years on the local police force. She was well acquainted with the mission of the Jane Carswell Home through interactions during her years as a member on the shelter board representing law enforcement. She was also well acquainted with Dr. Jane Carswell through the many victims they both knew. Jane answered Sharon's calls for help with sick clients. She kept tabs on the economic health of the shelter, making sure it was fiscally sound enough to continue.

For the executive directors, including current director, Lisa Clontz, the job became a mission. The safety, wellbeing, and future of the people they served were their responsibility, one not to take casually. They were the servants to those desperate for help. For Sharon Poarch, Dr. Carswell became a mentor who dropped by on occasion to sit down and talk, knowing the work was draining on the individual in charge. Jane described the shelter and its function in the community in her statement to the public:

Twenty-fifth Anniversary Celebration
2003

The Twenty Fifth Anniversary Celebration of the Shelter Home was a time for remembering and a time for pride at what the Shelter has accomplished, but even more important, a time to look forward into the future. From a vision of a few persons twenty-five years ago the Shelter Home has grown to employ seven full time and five part time persons. The program provides a safe haven for victims of domestic violence, counseling for many in the community who are not actual residents, aid for rape victims, and a preventive program in the county schools. Help with legal, financial, and housing needs is available.

In remembering, I mentioned a woman who arrived at the Shelter with five children who all wanted to sleep in the room with their mother as alerting us to the needs of children in homes of abuse. Imagine my surprise when after the program, a woman introduced herself as that woman who had received help twenty-five years ago! She now leads a happy and successful life and volunteers in a domestic violence agency.

I would personally like to thank everyone who helped make our Celebration such a success—Jan Pritchard and the former and present Image Players who presented the powerful drama "What's Love Got to do With It?", Jan Nash, our faithful volunteer who gave of her talent for singing, the City of Lenoir for allowing us free use of the Lenoir High Auditorium, James Messer with MDI for donating food, the news media for publicity, the Staff and Board of Directors of the Shelter, all of whom gave of their time and talents, and last but not least, all of the people who attended the event.

The Shelter Home has been successful not because of a few dedicated people but because of the support of the entire community. As we look forward to the future, we realize that much still needs to be done. In the past year one hundred forty-two women and ninety-two children found refuge in the Shelter, and an additional one thousand thirty-four received counseling. At the present with all the programs that we have and the economic situation as it is in our county, our financial needs are probably greater than they ever have been. We feel confident that support for the Shelter Home will be as outpouring in the future as it has been in the past.

After Dr. Carswell's death in March of 2015, the Shelter Home of Caldwell County's newsletter published a memorial edition dedicated to her and recognizing her work in being one of the founders of the shelter. An included photograph showed Jane receiving a Purple Ribbon Award in recognition for her years of dedicated and compassionate service for victims.

It also included a Bible verse that Jane lived by her entire life:

1 Corinthians 16:14 - Let all that you do be done in love.

From a plaque remembering the contribution Jane made,
forty years later, April 22, 2018

Shelter Home
of Caldwell County

SHELTER HOME OF CALDWELL COUNTY, INC.
PO BOX 426 • LENOIR, NC 28645

Peaceful Notes

JULY 2015

Board of Directors

Brent Phelps
Chair
Angie Clark
Vice-Chair
Ruth Kincaid
Secretary
Betsy Wilson
Treasurer

Bob Benfield
Kim Britt
Heidi Downs
Anita Dula
Debbie Eller
Chris Cole
Ann Kelly
Nancy Martin
Marla Parsons
Morris Reaves
Rose Reighard
Holly Yongue

Shelter Home Office
Phone Numbers:
Lenoir (828) 758-0888
Taylorsville (828) 635-8055

Crisis Lines:
Lenoir (828) 758-7088
Taylorsville (828) 635-8851
24 hours a day

Memorial Edition

Dr. Jane Carswell Roberts

(February 26, 1932 - March 25, 2015)

Through her patients, Jane witnessed a need to support victims of domestic violence and was a founding member of the Shelter Home of Caldwell County. She became one of the most committed volunteers.

Dr. Jane Carswell Roberts saw the results of violence and abuse in her medical practice in the mid-70s. She joined the commitment along with members of the First Presbyterian Church and the Caldwell Council on the Status of Women to end domestic violence and to serve victims of it. She served on the Board of Directors of the Shelter Home since 1993.

"Dr. Jane" received the "Purple Ribbon" recognition in 2013 for her years of dedicated & compassionate service for victims. Pictured left to right: Jan Nash, Nancy Martin, Dr. Jane Carswell Roberts, Ruth Kincaid and Betsy Wilson.

84

9

Caldwell House

"You can't cut patients off after office hours in a small town. They are people you go to church with, people you see in the grocery store. You have to be a part of the community."
Jane Carswell, *The Sandhill Citizen and News Outlook*
December 12, 1984

A major aspect of the success of the furniture industry in Caldwell County revolved around the semiannual furniture shows when buyers from across the country, and the world, browsed their way through showrooms displaying the latest designs. The frenzied weeks of preparation were capped with days of wining and dining the buyers, pitching the products, and taking orders. A good show meant an economic boom. A sluggish show meant potential layoffs. For several decades, individual showrooms dotted the landscape from High Point, North Carolina through Hickory and into Lenoir. During each spring and fall markets, buyers drove from one to the next in search of furnishing that fit their demands. After many years, that process simplified into a centralized market in High Point.

In the fifties, however, these buyers flocked to Lenoir during the furniture market. Industry leaders encouraged them to spend time viewing their latest offerings, but with only one motel in town for overnight stays, this time was limited. One enterprising company president, Hamilton Bruce, came up with a solution. His Hammary

Furniture Company built a sixteen bedroom rustic lodge to accommodate visiting buyers. His wife, Mary, the second half of the company's title, greeted the guests and served as hostess. Located on the top of a hill surrounded by a twelve acre tract of wooded land at the edge of the Lenoir city limits, "Kenham Lodge" offered both easy access to nearby showrooms and stunning mountain views in a relaxed environment.

By the mid-sixties, Hammary Furniture merged with an out of state company, and following Hamilton Bruce's untimely death in 1967, the lodge was no longer in use. It sat empty and available for the right person to come along.

He did.

He was John Christian Bernhardt, president of another furniture company in Lenoir, Bernhardt Industries. He was not in the hunt for a party lodge to entertain buyers, but as a leading member of a committee of concerned citizens, he was on the hunt for a facility for one specific purpose, a halfway house for recovering alcoholics.

The committee made up of industry leaders, ministers, lawyers, bankers, accountants and physicians banded together for the common cause of assisting those who had completed rehab, but were not ready to assimilate back into the community. Once recovering alcoholics were released from treatment centers, they typically returned to the environment where their addictions were a lifestyle. Without support, substance abuse often began again. Members of the committee were aware of these stumbling blocks through their own life experiences or from those they had witnessed in their daily encounters. The committee became a Board of Directors made up of fourteen people. They developed goals and guidelines based on the twelve-step program advocated by Alcoholics Anonymous and created five standing committees: finance, funding resources, housing and property, personnel and counselling, and public relations. They applied for state certification, while at the same time agreed not to accept state or federal funding or any kind of mental health grant money. "My billfold will keep this place going until it can go by itself," John Christian Bernhardt promised.

The day he stepped on the grounds at Kenham Lodge and saw the "For Sale" sign, Bernhardt realized this was the answer created to accomplish their dream. He made phone calls telling the others of his find. They spread out into the community looking for support. They went to businesses asking for donations. They went to civic organizations and churches. The two hundred forty thousand dollars needed to purchase the building was raised in two weeks, and their vision became a reality named Caldwell House. It had the potential to house thirty recovering addicts.

The first resident moved in Christmas Eve, 1983. The director was a recovering alcoholic, twelve years sober when he was hired. Although he had the heart and true desire for the job, he had no business experience. The pressure proved too great for him and he relapsed. Through the following years, other directors worked at Caldwell House. As issues developed, the board made suggestions for changes. Include drug addicts. Accept no client on medications that could be sold on the streets as drugs. Limit the resident clients to men only.

Caldwell House Front Gate

The current director, Bob Laws, was hired in 1993. Earlier in his life, Dr. Jane Carswell had recommended that he be committed to Broughton State Mental Hospital. On the day he met with the Caldwell House board for the job interview, he had to face her knowing she was fully aware of his past and that she was the same person who signed his commitment papers all those years ago. But he had traveled a long, difficult path since then. He once was a math teacher at a high school in the county until the day he was arrested during school hours on a cocaine charge. He lost his job and any hope for a career in teaching. He lost his family. He lost his freedom. He became a bitter felon, full of self-pity, angry at the world, but not at Dr. Carswell. She was kind, compassionate, but firm. He needed treatment and she helped make sure he got it.

He went through this treatment and ended up at Caldwell House in Al-Anon meetings on Sunday mornings, nine o'clock until ten, with a group of mothers dealing with family members' addictions. They sat in a circle in a small meeting room and poured out their hearts over the plague they were experiencing. He was on federal probation and was required to attend, but he resented being there. Yet these ladies never asked him to leave. They never told him to stop talking. He quit blaming others and began working on himself. Through it all, they loved him until he could love himself.

He plowed through issues and with help from some special sponsors, brought himself back into life as a recovering addict. He was employed as a plumber, resorting to the job that paid his way through college. He remarried. He took classes and earned certifications that allowed him to work in the mental health field as a substance abuse counselor. He worked at Safe Haven, a shelter in nearby Morganton which took in adolescents from tough, hard core situations. These teens attended therapy sessions and Alcoholics Anonymous meetings with him. Many of them needed significant medical care, and Bob recommended a lady doctor in Lenoir, Dr. Carswell. He began referring the teens to her, overloading her with them, yet she never turned them down.

So he knew about Jane Carswell before he ever knew Jane Carswell. That knowledge came after he was hired as the Executive Director of Caldwell House. That's when he learned, as he said about Jane, "She could have walked with lepers."

This walk brought her to the facility often, her arms usually overloaded with donated copies of *National Geographic* or *Reader's Digest*. Hers was the voice overwhelmed clients and their families at the Al-Anon Sunday sessions waited to hear. Hers was the calming voice board members needed to heed. She was able to recognize the good in people and look through all the harshness. She had no prejudgments, no exclusions.

> **HOUSE STATISTICS**
> (As of Feb. 25, 2015)
>
> Residents----------20
> Number working fulltime----16
> (Others do pick-up jobs when possible and also do volunteer work.)
> Where residents came from
>   North Carolina-------18
>   Maryland-------------1
>   Wisconsin------------1

Jane agreed with Bob that the four-month limit on residency was not long enough. The men needed time to heal. Those who came to Caldwell House were broken from terrific problems associated with addiction. They had family issues, and they came out of treatment not knowing where to go. Their health had been compromised with heart trouble or liver problems, or their teeth and gums had been destroyed. They carried tremendous legal and financial problems from when they had resorted to selling drugs or stealing to buy their own drugs on the streets. Many of them were convicted felons. No matter how hard they tried, they could not put the parts of their lives back together quickly. Although they were no longer using, their recovery was slow. The four-month rule was rewritten, and men were allowed to stay as long as they were making progress.

While private donations accounted for half the costs of operating Caldwell House, the other half came from the weekly fee paid by the residents, a hundred thirty-five dollars. Some churches sponsored men who could not afford to pay on their own. Others paid for the first month for men just coming out of prison. Those who couldn't pay and were not ready to enter the work force when they first arrived were assigned volunteer tasks to help at a food bank or other community sponsored organizations. As their lives settled and their health began to restore, they were required to take jobs out in the community, yet they had no cars and usually had suspended licenses to drive. They depended on Caldwell House for transportation.

Jane remained connected to Caldwell House for many years, serving as a board member and then later as the editor of the Caldwellian, a quarterly newsletter that kept families and donors connected to the activities of the house. Each edition included a column written by Jane featuring an inspiring story of a client living in the home. She paid attention to details so that she could write the articles authentically, using the language and identifying mannerisms that were unique to addicts, always double checking with the individuals for their approval of the articles before publication. Betsy McRee formatted the newsletter, and the graphic arts class at Hibriten High School published it.

Bob Laws keeps a word on his desk. *Ahimsa.* It is from Sanskrit, translating, "Do No Harm." He tries to remember that word all day, every day as he works with addicts. He knows one of them might possibly kill himself, but yet another one won't, and that is why he continues. He knows the difference Caldwell House makes in lives.

Dr. Jane Carswell knew it, too.

THE CALDWELLIAN

| Caldwell House | Volume 11 | Issue 2 | May, 2015 |

This issue is dedicated to the memory of
Dr. Jane Carswell Roberts
February 26, 1932—March 25, 2015

Dr. Jane Carswell Roberts

CONDOLENCES

The board, staff and Caldwell House Community wishes to express sincere sympathy to Kenneth Roberts and Family in the loss of his wife, Dr. Jane Carswell Roberts.

She was a faithful supporter of the House for many years, served on the board and edited this newsletter and we feel a real loss also.

MEMORIES OF JANE

About 25 years ago I was working for a branch of Foothills Mental Health which dealt with adolescent females. Most had great needs and no resources. Someone told me about a Dr. Jane Carswell who might see one of these girls so I sent one of these needy clients to her office without any warning whatsoever. Dr. Carswell treated her with love and kindness. This encouraged me so much that I eventually sent the rest of these unwanted clients.

Many years later I went to work at the Caldwell House and to my surprise this dear lady was one of the board members. I immediately thought that she is going to get me for sending her all of those freeloaders. Over the next couple of decades I was able to personally observe this kind and gentle lady quietly and humbly go about serving this entire community as the need arose .She was truly an example of one who could walk with and serve the lepers.

She later retired and married Ken Roberts, but as Ken soon discovered his bride was even busier than before she retired. I won't even attempt to list the numerous services which she continued until her death, but I am so glad that I was privileged to have such a wonderful mentor to lead me through the world of serving others.

Dr. Jane left a huge hole in our needy little community. As a way to show respect to Jane, I am going to try harder to live up to her wonderful example.

Respectfully,
**Bob Laws,
Director of the Caldwell House**

From Rose Reighard:

Rose Reighard remembers when Dr Jane got married. When the minister said "Who gives this woman?" 5 or 6 nephews spoke up on her behalf. Rose went on tour to Germany with her and realized she was an avid bird watcher.

Rose also remembers all the areas in Lenoir she had worked, giving her time and specialties; "Who will replace her, go under bridges treating the homeless?" Who will go to the Shelter Home? Who will provide free medical care at the clinic?

Who will go to Leo's, the new homeless shelter?

Who will show the support she provided to the Caldwell House?

She is not someone who can be replaced.

****

From Jenny Kent, Board Member

I met Dr. Jane when she came to my house to interview me for the Caldwellian. I had just joined the Board, and she wanted to introduce me. As we talked, and shared a little about each other, I quickly learned we had something in common and we had a heart for those who struggled with addiction.

Shortly after that meeting, she started picking up my son from the Caldwell House, and having him help with her church's food pantry. The encouragement she gave my son, and me, was priceless. I felt like she loved him when others did not want anything to do with him. We've lost a sweet dear friend, whom I'm so happy was a part of our lives. I know this is not good bye….but just see you later!

****

From Lory Dansky, Caldwell House Board Secretary

When I think back about Jane, two words come to mind - service and humility. Knowing just some of the service she offered to so many individuals and so many organizations, almost overwhelms me. And to remember how she served, so quietly, easily, and always with a gentle smile.

Actually, the word that most fills my heart is gratitude. All our gratitude for the life of a humble servant.

10

Caldwell Friends

"Family physicians have a responsibility in the community.
Because we are on the front line,
the problems often come first into our offices."
Jane Carswell, speaking to the Delegates
Assembly American Association of Physicians,
AAFP Reporter, October 1984

 Dr. Jane Carswell, like all cradle-to-grave doctors, provided medical care to every stage from pre-birth to senior citizens, not forgetting the vulnerable teen years. Jane's compassion for that group brought her to be involved in several organizations in Caldwell County specifically designed to help teens avoid a future of crime.

One of the organizations where she had significant input was Pioneer Home, a residential home for troubled youth. The thirteen to fifteen year old boys who lived at the home were sent there by the court system as an alternative to juvenile detention. They were in legal jeopardy, and needed a community to offer them help through structure and counseling. Jane encouraged churches to support the boys, to visit them on holidays or to celebrate birthdays with them, and to be the encouragers that these boys never had. After a few years the local group home was absorbed by a business corporation of group homes that eventually phased out their operation in Caldwell County.

Seeking answers to juvenile crime prevention drew Governor Jim Hunt into developing the Governor's One-on-One Program in 1983. Each county in North Carolina developed a plan as a part of the program. The one created in Lenoir was in response to a need seen by professionals in the court system and by a number of concerned citizens, including Dr. Carswell. It resulted in Caldwell Friends, a local, independent program based on the big brother, big sister concept. A mentor was matched with a "high risk" youth for a one year period of time and asked to devote at least two hours a week spending time with them as a friend. Most often these boys and girls came from a bad home situation and were in need of positive role models. Jane served on the steering committee and gave input into how the program could be effective. She and other community leaders formed a board of directors and hired Cathy Swanson as the first director. Cathy made presentations at churches and civic organizations, not only asking for donations, but recruiting volunteers.

Funding came from the state's Juvenile Crime Prevention Council, local Broyhill, Coffey, and Bernhardt Foundations, personal donations, and fund raisers. Before Christmas one year Jane invited several of her friends to a "snowflake bee" in her home to make ornaments to raise money for Caldwell Friends. Another fundraiser was a raffle with a grand prize of three thousand, five hundred dollars. Jane held the winning ticket and donated all the money back. A few years after its inception, North Carolina experienced a budget crisis and the One-on-One program was eliminated. Because of the community's support coupled with additional funding from Juvenile Crime Prevention Council, Caldwell Friends was able to remain a vital tool for responding to the needs of children throughout the county. In 1985 Caldwell Friends became a part of United Way.

Jane drew a picture of mascot Raydell holding a bouquet of flowers on her thank you note to director Cathy Swanson.

The ages of children accepted into the program varied from as young as seven up to those seventeen years of age, although currently to those fourteen years old. Most children had been adjudicated by a juvenile court as undisciplined or delinquent, committing a crime such as truancy that an adult would not be charged with. The objective was to impact them with a positive role model before their crimes escalated. The plan was to offer stable, adult guidance on a personal level. The goal was to improve home and school performance and behavior, social skills, and peer relations, and to decrease contact with law enforcement. The tag line was "Your time will make a difference." The symbol was an hour glass.

Photograph provided by Caldwell Friends

Left to right, John O'Connor, Betsy Wilson, Jane, Charles Brady receiving hour glasses in recognition of their many hours devoted to Caldwell Friends

Volunteer mentors went through extensive background checks and training before being matched with a child. They arranged a schedule to meet on a weekly basis, after school hours or on weekends, giving the child a personal resource outside the family. Often the fathers were incarcerated. Many of the children were living with grandparents. The vast majority were from economically disadvantaged families.

In 1989 WSOC-TV in Charlotte awarded Caldwell Friends one of its annual "Nine Who Care" Awards for supporting the children in the county. Each year, the Channel Nine television station recognized nine organizations in its viewing region for significant service to their communities. Executive director at the time, Gwin Laws, spoke about the program, as quoted by the Lenoir *News-Topic*, "They [mentors] can make a difference between a person choosing a life of crime and becoming a good citizen and maybe even a leader in the community."

Caldwell Friends is located in the Fidelity Building in uptown Lenoir. Executive Director currently is Liz Eller and Program Administrator is Susan Rudisill. With a grant from the Bernhardt Foundation, local folk artist, Charlie Frye worked with several of the clients to create a mural on the lobby wall. He outlined puzzle pieces that individual children painted depicting putting the pieces of the puzzle of their lives back together, their goals, and what they wanted to be when they grew up. He centered it around a gigantic hour glass, with the mentor making time and the child planning all the way through graduation. This mural became a visual reminder of the aim of Caldwell Friends, to offer dreams of a future. At the top he included a bird to represent the desire of staff and mentors alike, for the children to successfully soar and make their dreams come true.

Image courtesy of Charlie Frye and Folk Keeper Gallery

11

International Missions

"The Guatemalan mothers with sick children
showed the same anxiety and love that I see in parents
in my office in North Carolina."
Jane Carswell, "Reflections on Guatemala Trip"
February 4, 2002

 In her daily walk being a servant of God by being a servant to God's people, Jane sought out ways to help others beyond the Caldwell County lines. She traveled with a delegation to Nicaragua in 1993. Their goal was to learn about the work of the Presbyterian church in Nicaragua and to help build a dormitory on the Young Life farm/camp near Matagalpa. For ten days they visited various rural projects and worked on the cooperative farm. They witnessed the church alive. They also witnessed firsthand the reality of living in a nation in turmoil.

One evening at La Vida Joven, a farm and camp where they had been working in the fields, they gathered in the dining area for devotions. Just as

Photograph provided by
Western Carolina Presbytery Archives
**Jane working the fields in
Nicaragua**

they ended, four armed men dressed in military fatigues appeared at the door and told them they "needed to get outside in a line."

Two of the men remained guarding them while the other two went inside, and gathered things of value including money, passports, and unfortunately, Jane's beloved camera. The men then went to each person present, lightly touching the backs of their necks in search of gold chains. They told them to return inside, saying to them, "No tenga miedo" (don't be afraid). Then they left, taking their loot, taking Jane's camera. No one was harmed physically, but the group was frightened at this realization of the seriousness of poverty in Nicaragua.

Photograph provided by Judith Nebrig

**The Nicaragua Mission team,
Jane kneeling, first on left**

The entire night they remained together in fear that the men who robbed them would return. They talked and prayed, sharing with each other their reactions to what they were enduring. Jane later told friends in Lenoir that although she did not know if she were going to die, she felt a peace that if she lived or died, she was where she needed to be. Judith Nebrig, one of the several huddled behind closed doors, wrote that Jane was a calming presence during that experience. The next morning when the sun rose they sang, with much "gusto and gratitude," and a new appreciation of the words, "When Morning Gilds the Skies…May Jesus Christ Be Praised!"

Their written report ended with these words:

This experience underscores the lack of support available for public institutions in Nicaragua. We think it significant that we experienced this incident with Nicaraguan Christians who will continue their work in order to offer an alternative to young men like those who robbed us. It is also significant that they did not harm us, nor raise their voices. We hope and pray that our experience with our Christian brothers and sisters in Nicaragua will precipitate not a retreat from, but more response to, and support for the work of the Christians in the small post-war struggling country.

When the Western North Carolina Presbytery entered into a covenant relationship with two Presbyteries in Central America's Guatemala, Jane wanted to participate. This partnership agreement set out to change the established model for mission where people from first world, wealthy countries came to poor, underdeveloped countries, bringing their customs, ideas, and traditions to teach, evangelize, heal and help people. Those who gave money often controlled both the giving and the use of the money, creating a system of dependence and passivity of people. A covenant would be different, a mutual partnership that would respond to many elements, including health care.

Photograph provided by Western Carolina Presbytery Archives

Mission planning session: Seated Left to Right, Judy Nebrig, Norma Bleander, Phyllis Simeon; Standing, Jane Carswell, Lorrie Shelly, Melinda Wilson, Ed McFadden, Marilyn Marks, Steve Owens

The initial core group designing the health component included Robert Moore, who was fluent in Spanish and would later serve as a missionary in Guatemala, Dr. Douglas Michael a family physician practicing in Conover, North Carolina, Trel Lowe, a nurse practitioner who would later serve a term as a missionary on the Mexican border, and Dr. Jane Carswell. In addition to those four in America, the committee was composed of two representatives from each of the two Presbyteries in Guatemala. They met on a regular basis to prepare for the initiation of the ministry. One of the concerns that this committee expressed time and again was their desire that this project be a ministry that continued beyond their short visits. They sought to work together and learn about each other as partners rather than imposing one system of medical care on the other.

The primary language in Guatemala, Spanish, was spoken by only sixty percent of the people. The remaining population spoke one of the officially recognized twenty-three different dialects in the native indigenous tongue. Beyond language limitations, the team faced a cultural barrier between them and the team in Guatemala.

Thirty churches in the Western North Carolina Presbytery became involved in the partnership. The two Presbyteries in Guatemala, Sur Occidente and Suchitepequez, were rural and comprised of mainly indigenous heritages. Teams on both halves of the covenant were determined to live out Paul's words that "in Christ there is neither Jew nor Greek, slave nor free, men or women, but we are one in Christ," as well as his words that we are to "encourage one another in the faith." However, as Dr. Michael writes,

The theology relating faith and Christian service was not well-developed in Guatemala, and often the two were deemed mutually exclusive. The acknowledged health needs were often secondary to other processes that were not appreciated (i.e. poverty, educational deficits, inadequate public heath infrastructure), and gender issues were both obvious to us Americans and dealt with only indirectly. Our Guatemalan partners were often seeing large numbers of female elders, and in our committee, female physicians and advanced health care professionals for the first time.

In the past, the mission of the Presbyterian Church emphasized the promises of God for life after this life and the church struggled to define its mission in relation to the promises of God for life in the here and now. The health project was considered one indication of the "vida abundante" (abundant life) that God promised through Jesus Christ for His people in the present.

Jane's first visit to Guatemala was with the team in January of 1996. For ten days they met with the pastors and laypersons in the two areas, and visited health care facilities, asking questions and discussing problems with pastors and community leaders. Although their mission was to evaluate needs to determine future plans, they provided some medical care when an immediate need was obvious. Dr. Michael remembers Jane being "the first to jump up, investigate, and take care of any medical problem that came to our attention."

They became aware of issues facing individuals in the country, land distribution, racial discrimination against the indigenous population and urgent social needs that could be addressed by health care. The consensus of the groups was that their work together would be a health promoter training project to focus on prevention, health promotion and basic curative measures. Two promoters from each Guatemalan church in the Presbyteries would be trained so they could serve basic health needs in their communities. Jane attended regular meetings of the group in North Carolina and participated in additional trips to Guatemala. In 1997 they held medical clinics and modeled health care for the promoters-in-training. In 1998 they celebrated those who completed their first year of training. In 2000 they held workshops to help promoters identify the most urgent community health needs and from that visit, home garden, nutrition, and clean water initiatives were developed. Jane wrote a skit about the importance of health promotion for the team to perform in Guatemala. Although the tense political situation in Guatemala had ended a decades-long civil war in 1996 with peace accords, reports of violence continued. Fortunately Jane and the team experienced none during her several visits.

But then there was the road situation, writes Dr. Michael. The roads in Guatemala were largely potholes. Virtually every leg of every trip involved a "pinchazo" (flat tire) on one the pickups driven by the Guatemalan hosts who "served not only as chauffeurs, but also as guides, guardians, language instructors, givers-and-sharers-of-all-they-had, friends and brothers," (and sisters, adds Virginia Stevens). Travelling on major roads, at forty miles per hour, meant slowing abruptly for potholes or tumulos (large speed bumps). Team members stood unrestrained in the back of the pickups while the driver swerved to wherever the road was smoothest. Periodically, someone in the back would become anxious, pound on the roof of the cab, and complain about driving on the wrong side of the road.

Years later Jane wrote a series of articles about the Guatemala Partnership that shared not only her experiences, but her desire to be the hands and feet of Jesus for the world:

Guatemalan Woman
March 15, 2000

Up in the chilly dawn at 4 a.m. she balances her basket of corn upon her head. With grace of a ballet dancer she travels the well-worn dirt path to the Molina [gas powered machine to grind corn]. Some of the monopoly-like money is paid to have the corn ground for the life-sustaining tortillas.

Upon returning home she is greeted by proud roosters announcing the day and their own importance. Wood gathered the day before is lit. Her hands, as skilled as any potters, shapes perfect thin circles of the ground maize.

Acrid smoke belches forth from the open fire. My unaccustomed eyes stream water, and the heat in the small palm thatched room resembles Dante's Inferno. Deftly the white, flat disks are turned by a quick movement of her hand—no fancy kitchen utensils for her.

An eight year old beauty with dark eyes and skinny legs joins her mother and draws water from the well. No windlass here, just a rope, a single pulley and strong arms bring up bucket after bucket.

Black beans and tortillas provide energy for the day's unending tasks. The men and children fed and the baby nursed, the grueling day has just begun. Clothes pounded on rocks in the muddy river turn miraculously white. The sharp creases after ironing belie the fact that this is done with a flatiron. Corn and a few other vegetables are tended as the noonday sun beats relentlessly down on arms in constant motion.

Where does her strength come from to do these tasks which are unending? Perhaps the church. The family goes together Sundays and several days during the week. The prayers, the praise, the hymns, the readings and the preached Word of God undergird her life.

But perhaps a vital strength is also laughter. Part of the laughter is brought about by the games these people from the States with their awkward sounding Spanish brought with them. All become children—the women, men, the foreigners, and the children. The free range pigs and chickens seem to be joining in the fun. London Bridge is falling down. "Todas Las Frutas" shouted turns the Fruit Basket Over.

There is grand confusion and mingling of many bodies and deep, freely offered laughter. The day's labors are left outside for a brief period.

The laughter probably does help make it bearable. And for myself, it makes the disparity of our lives more bearable. I too can forget and laugh for a short time. Thanks be to God for laughter!

Photograph provided by
Western Carolina Presbytery Archives

Guatemalan Partnership Banner

Reflections on Guatemalan Trip
February 4, 2002

My initial reaction to the whole trip is that life is unfair. Why do some people who work extremely hard, and probably are better Christians than I am, not have many of the essentials of life?

I have since realized that the important thing is not the question, but the response of Christians who have more, to the problems of inequality. To whom much is given, much is expected.

The Guatemalan mothers with sick children showed the same anxiety and love that I see in parents in my office in North Carolina. An elderly man describing the anguish he felt when his wife died related the same symptoms we see in someone going through the grieving process here— anger, not eating, not sleeping, withdrawing from people.

The Christian church responded in ways that we would have—took him food, visited him, let him talk of his loss, and prayed for him and with him. We are much more alike than different.

On my last trip to Guatemala I was "The Game Lady," as I had charge of the recreation. One of the most rewarding things for me was to see the older people forget their hard life for at least a short time and play and laugh as children. We had gone as the Healthcare Provider team. Mental and spiritual health need to be ministered to as well as physical well-being.

History of our Guatemala Partnership
February 19, 2014

The Presbytery's partnership began in 1994, but Presbyterian's interest in Guatemala began in the 1800's. With Spain's loss of control of Central America, Protestant groups met to see how they could make inroads into mainly Catholic countries and also bring the message of the Gospel to persons practicing native Indian religions. The countries were divided up, and the Presbyterians ended up with Guatemala.

In the 1990's people began seeking ways the Presbyterians there and those in the United States could support each other: "that we may be mutually encouraged by each other's faith." (Romans 1:12). In 1994 a partnership agreement was signed. Since then many churches in the Presbytery of Western North Carolina have developed a partnership with a sister church in the presbyteries of Sur Occidente and Suchitepequez (Sur and Suchi). Letters, pictures, musical recordings, and other tangible things have been shared. Our church sent a communion cup made by a local potter to our sister church with their and our names on it. We have prayed for each other, especially in times of trouble, including natural disasters such as earthquakes and hurricanes, and during political violence. Guatemalans prayed for us, especially at 9-11.

At the request of Guatemalans in 1996 a Health Team from the Presbytery of Western North Carolina visited churches of both presbyteries to see what they wanted regarding health care. I was a member of that group. We listened to them about their needs and they heard from us what we thought feasible. It was decided to train two health providers in each church. The health providers would be trained to educate people about proper sanitation, the importance of clean drinking water, good nutrition especially for children and pregnant women, and other health concerns. The health providers learned to take temperatures and blood pressures and were able to give advice as to when help from a medical doctor was needed. A few people were suspicious when they couldn't see the "germs" we talked about under the old microscope that someone had left there many years ago. Geny Merida, a Guatemalan medical student whose father was the moderator of the General Assembly in Guatemala, was able to convince them that germs really existed and caused illnesses.

Community health projects have developed. Among these are vegetable and medicinal gardens, composting latrines, fuel efficient stoves, and others. One member of United Presbyterian Church in Lenoir asked that people remember her husband by giving gifts in his memory to a church in Guatemala for a community garden. Enough money was given to clear an acre of land and plant a garden. The Health Ministry is supported by the 5 cents a Meal program.

The Education Program began with scholarships for lay ministers in Guatemala to the seminary there. Members of Fairview Presbyterian gave money for some of these as alternative gifts. The idea for scholarships for children actually began in Lenoir. Jose Coto, a father of four, was a member of the sister church of Quaker Meadows and First Presbyterian Church of Lenoir. He knew that children needed education to get jobs and when he visited Lenoir asked for help with this. Guidelines were finally worked out. Fairview began furnishing $50 scholarships for 50 children yearly in 2008. The money helps buy books, school supplies, uniforms, shoes, and sometimes transportation. Two girls from our sister church are now in high school.

We thank God for what the Guatemala Partnership has meant to all of us and look to Him for guidance in our future together. May we all continue to grow in our faith and love for one another.

*Jane celebrating her sixty-eighth birthday in 2000
on a mission trip to Guatemala.*

12

Helping Hands

***"The family physician is in a unique position to work for better
health care for the community on a broad scale."***
Jane Carswell, *Family Practice Hi-Lights*,
Medical College of Virginia Student Family Practice Association
Winter, 1984

 Perhaps one of the most frustrating aspects of family practice that Jane expressed vocally was in dealing with medical injustices and affordable health care. Too often she treated a patient and wrote a prescription only to find later that patient could not afford to fill the prescription. In many cases, Jane paid for patients' necessary medications out of her own pocket. Other physicians shared similar concerns. They often treated patients in their offices or at the emergency room and expected them to follow through with their recommended care, only to have them return in a few days with the same symptoms that had, by then, compounded with lack of proper treatment. Prescriptions meant nothing as long as the clients had no access to affordable medication. Many times these were the elderly patients who lived on a fixed income and were covered by government sponsored Medicare, which for the first years of its existence, had no drug supplement option.

The concern was great enough that it was discussed in the early nineties by the Healthy Caldwellians, a group funded by North

Carolina Healthy Carolinians with Debi Nelson as executive director. This local unit was partnered with the UNC Center for Health Promotion and Disease Prevention and received funding from Duke Endowment. "What if," they conjectured, "volunteers, particularly those from the medical field, could organize a way to help, to give a hand, and to address the need for proper medical treatment for people who had no resources to pay for it?"

This free clinic they suggested would serve those citizens of Caldwell County Jane was so insistent to provide for: the seniors, or those unemployed who had no way of paying for treatment, much less for their medications, or those who were working, but could not afford the high cost of the group insurance policies their employers offered and faced the difficult choice between placing a meal on the table or paying an insurance premium.

What the group could give this population was a helping hand and what this group needed was a name. They chose one – Helping Hands Clinic.

The committee found an unused space in the basement below Medical Arts Pharmacy, a drug store located across the street from the hospital. They wrote grants and were partially funded by Caldwell Memorial Hospital, United Way of Caldwell County, Duke Endowment, the North Carolina Community Foundation, and the North Carolina Department of Health and Human Services. Jane made phone calls, realizing as in the other humanitarian projects she supported, people with money and the ability to help were not always aware these problems existed, or if they were, how they could help. The community responded in an overwhelming way. They opened their purse strings and they signed up to volunteer. With this money, the clinic hired Executive Director Karen Phoenix and opened for Caldwell County residents in August, 1998.

Hospital social worker at the time, Terri Looper Niederhammer tells about their pride the day the clinic first opened, calling it "not even grassroots, but weeds of a little organization." Terri was the volunteer in charge of social work, teaching those who would be screening potential clients to determine eligibility, and writing that particular section of the protocol and procedures manual. Jane and a few other doctors wrote the medical guidelines. Patients who had been in the emergency room and were given a prescription, but could not afford to purchase the medication, were eligible to be served by the clinic. Physicians referred patients to fill prescriptions. Others came through the Department of Social Services. The Lenoir *News-Topic* ran several articles publicizing the clinic and its Tuesday/Thursday, five thirty until nine evening hours. Some people walked in off the street seeking help, and the clinic became their primary source for medical care. It served patients who needed short term immediate help with antibiotics, and patients who needed long term chronic care, some who were "brittle" diabetics, who, with no finances to purchase blood sugar medicine, had gotten to the point where they had severe neuropathy or kidney failure. The clinic dealt with COPD, congestive heart failure, hypertension, and allergies, supplying acute and chronic medications, although never narcotics. There was an open door policy that always found a way to provide care once the person's income was verified as needing assistance. However, the clinic saw very few children, as most lower-income families qualified for Medicaid for their children.

The clinic was in an ideal location across the road from the hospital where those needing a helping hand could come directly from the emergency room for prescriptions, or where specimens could quickly be transferred to a lab at the hospital. But the location was not in an ideal building. The space was cramped with two exam rooms, a tiny lobby and a reception area. The in-house pharmacy was converted from an old, dingy, poorly-lit room into a newer, cleaner, poorly-lit room. The boiler room, with its still functioning boiler, became the lab that included a dorm sized refrigerator to store specimens when necessary. Opposite that room was an even smaller "break" room.

Dr. John McMenemy and Dr. Jim Gardner volunteered to be the first medical directors and worked alongside several volunteer pharmacists, nurses and lab technicians. With more grants, Helping Hands was able to pay a part time pharmacist. They recruited volunteers from churches and civic organizations in addition to the professional community. The first Christmas after Helping Hands opened was a celebration. Several of the patients, staff and board members held an impromptu party, decorating a tree in the tiny lobby, and enjoying snacks furnished by Jane and other volunteers. Many patients brought small gifts, food, anything to say thank you, as in the beginning there was no charge for any services. By the third year they began asking for a five dollar monthly donation fee from those who could pay as a way for them to give back.

Debi Nelson designed the clinic logo based on Jane's concept, a pair of hands cupping a heart and displaying the medical symbol of a winged rod and serpent. Although it has been replaced with a newer logo, this original logo still graces the awning above the pharmacy's front entrance, donated by Annas Awnings, a company in Hickory, North Carolina.

Because the clinic was open after hours, many volunteers came directly from work without time for an evening meal. The staff sent out a request for meal donations, and churches throughout the county responded by supplying easy to eat on the run, nutritious meals for the volunteers. Beyond those in the medical profession, volunteers came from all backgrounds imaginable. They learned how to file records. They were trained to assist the pharmacy technicians. They became patient advocates who completed necessary paperwork to send to pharmaceutical companies requesting medications at no or reduced costs. They cared for an increasing number of clients, more than doubling in size.

With success came growing pains as the number of clients and the need outpaced the size of the basement location. A storefront business a few blocks away in downtown Lenoir closed and the building was placed on the market. Once again Helping Hands wrote grants for donations. With the help of foundations such as Duke Endowment, they eventually purchased this three story building. The timing was perfect for building donations from one important source, Blackwelder Hospital. Debi Nelson recalls that it had closed and Helping Hands was given the opportunity to take anything they needed from the facility. Several large, wooded doors were "harvested" from the exam rooms, as well as counters for the pharmacy and other usable materials. In addition, the estate of Dr. Raymond D. Wallace, a local physician, donated medical equipment, exam tables, cabinets, stools and file cabinets. All these donations enabled Helping Hands to keep the costs down. Tim Bentley of Bentley Construction remodeled the building and donated much of the materials he used.

The dedication for the new facility was in March 2002 and at that point, the clinic changed from two evenings a week to four days a week, opening from eight in the morning until six in the evening. Another change was in response to a need for consistency in medical care so that clients could be seen by the same physician at each visit. With more grant money, Helping Hands Clinic hired a part-time, retired physician, Dr. Andrew Metzger. At the same time, it began CHAP, the Caldwell Health Access Program that paired uninsured patients with volunteer doctors who did not come on site at Helping Hands, but saw patients in their own offices and sent prescriptions to the clinic to be processed. Access to chronic disease management care was essential for these patients.

President George W. Bush signed the Medicare Prescription Drug Improvement and Modernization Act in late 2003 addressing one of the original purposes for the creation of the Helping Hands Clinic, medication for seniors. When Medicare Part D became implemented in North Carolina, seniors once again turned to their own physicians and pharmacies for care. Helping Hands was then able to devote more resources to the uninsured population that had quite suddenly increased throughout the county. One by one over a period of four or five years, the furniture companies, long the economic base for employment in Caldwell County, began to outsource to cheaper labor costs abroad, and an estimated ten thousand jobs were eliminated locally. A worker who once earned fifteen to eighteen dollars an hour with full benefits became unemployed with no medical insurance to rely on. Helping Hands responded by enrolling those workers, often going into the shops before they closed and pre-enrolling those who would be impacted.

By this time, Jane had retired from her practice, yet she maintained her medical license in order to volunteer in the clinic as well as at other humanitarian programs she was involved with. She renewed her malpractice insurance yearly, paying the cost herself. She also paid for any required licensing fees. At the clinic she often provided care to patients she had once seen in her practice.

According to Assistant Executive Director Debra Philyaw, Helping Hands Clinic operates as a primary care practice that sees about eighteen hundred patients in a year's time with more than another three hundred patients in the CHAP program. The pharmacy fills over twenty thousand prescriptions per year. The clinic employs seven full time staff members and several part-time physicians and physician assistants under supervising doctor, Dr. Denise Herman, a retired physician. A full time pharmacy technician runs the pharmacy. Approximately thirty to thirty-five volunteers work in the clinic weekly,

the majority in the pharmacy.

Jane's influence at Helping Hands is on exhibit from the front lobby. Beyond a door to the left are plaques listing Jane as among those honored as the 1998 founding board members and among those leaders behind the 2002 new clinic building. On the wall to

Image courtesy of Charlie Frye and Folk Keeter Gallery

the right is a mural by Lenoir Folk Artist, Charlie Frye, depicting a doctor reminiscent of Jane standing with a patient.

When Jane died in 2015, Executive Director Lilly Bunch organized a small memorial ceremony at the clinic honoring her with a proclamation by the board of directors recognizing her for "her commitment to others, her civic engagement and her tireless efforts on behalf of those in need...her strong advocacy for the issues she held dear, and especially for her commitment to medical access for all and the patients of Helping Hands Clinic."

Below the proclamation hangs this picture of Jane and Kenneth Roberts taken at the clinic's annual "Pot of Gold" fundraiser.

13

Cradle-to-Grave

*"I would love to give you back your good health but cannot.
So I will give you my love, which you have always had.
May you feel God's arms around you
and know the peace that only He can give."*
Jane Carswell in a letter to a friend

 Anticipating her future retirement, Jane bought land next to her sister, Jill, on Mirror Lake in Providence Forge, Virginia where she planned to build a small house and eventually relocate. Although she had developed deep friendships in her life in Lenoir, this family-oriented physician witnessed an important end-of-life value time and again. "When you are at the end of life, you need to be with relatives," she said. "Friends are important, but relatives are needed." She had options. Many of her patients facing end-of-life decisions did not.

Seniors living alone, many of them under Dr. Carswell's care, typically could not maintain a safe and healthy standard of living without assistance. In many cases, there was no help available. A spouse might have died or family members moved out of the area, leaving their elderly isolated and dependent on the goodness of neighbors. Cooking meals for themselves was often a neglected chore. Upkeep on a home was a task many could not manage themselves nor afford to pay others. Realizing this was a crisis that needed attention, in June of 1974 First Presbyterian Church offered office space to the Retired Senior Volunteer Program (RSVP). This group sponsored the local Meals-on-Wheels program, a mid-day meal delivery service to the home bound. In 1979 they built a small kitchen facility where meals were prepared not only to deliver to the disabled and elderly in their homes and to government sponsored day care centers, but also to serve those who came into the facility off the streets, a forerunner of the Lenoir Soup Kitchen.

That alleviated the nutritional dangers of aging, but Jane recognized proper housing still was an issue, and brought these concerns to Rev. Williamson. With her encouragement and his leadership, they found segments within the congregation who would take up the cause. After many discussions, the committee determined a retirement home for senior citizens was the most pressing need. The church pledged to support it until it could reach self-sustaining status. According to Lucy McCarl's history of the First Presbyterian Church in Lenoir, *You Shall Be My People*, Dr. Verne Blackwelder approached them with an offer. He owned a building in Lenoir he was willing to donate, an old hotel, the Carlheim, within walking distance of the church.

Built by Dr. A. F. Houck in 1899 as the first hospital in Lenoir, it never actually opened as a medical facility. Nancy Alexander in her book, *A Medical History of Caldwell County*, stated that the "hospital could not succeed at a time when such a facility was an innovation, and it was too difficult for one doctor to operate." It was converted into the Lenoir Inn, and later became the Carlheim Hotel. Its elegant beauty had deteriorated over the years and by the time the Presbyterian Church took ownership, it was beyond repair to update and meet newer building codes. Church members sold all the furnishing from the hotel in a yard sale, and the hotel was demolished. In 1976 the Department of Housing and Urban Development approved the church's application for a two and a half million dollar grant for housing for senior citizens.

A ground breaking for the new building at the hotel site was held December 18, 1977 and a dedication service for the finished building on October 14, 1979. Between those dates, a name was selected for the apartments, Koinonia, a Greek word that describes a fellowship and sharing similar to that of the early Christians in the book of Acts. Two additional Presbyterian churches in Lenoir, Fairview and United, joined with First Church in sponsoring this retirement home. Although Jane was not as involved during the organizing process, she later supported the project in many ways. She visited the seniors who had moved into the eighty-two efficiency apartments in the building. She

Koinonia

made "apartment" calls. She brought roses. She cared for her seniors.

She cared for them, too, as they entered into the final years of their lives. Dr. Jane Carswell understood that dying was a part of living. She felt there were better ways to die than taking extraordinary measures to keep the heart beating longer when quality of life was gone.

Her nephew, Robert Carswell wrote about a death and dying discussion he had with Jane:

A conversation with Jane was often thought provoking. I was perhaps not very polished in presenting my views, but she listened patiently. In one conversation when I was in my early twenties, we discussed euthanasia (Dr. Jack Kevorkian was in the news) and I was looking for her to provide a definitive opinion on the topic, but I walked away with something else to think about. She said that to fear death and sickness would be misinterpreting life. That turned the conversation on its end. She also said the simple rules that people seem to crave often divert us from seeing the broader picture. I was stumped again.

During a family night event at First Presbyterian Church the congregation was introduced to the Hospice concept, a movement taking hold across the nation. The speaker, registered nurse Catherine Respess [Barnes], had attended the Third Annual North Carolina Hospice Conference with a grant from the church and was reporting what she had learned. Jane immediately recognized a solution to her concerns and invited Rev. Williamson, speaker Catherine Respess, and a few others who had expressed an interest in Hospice to her home the following week to discuss possibilities. From this initial gathering, a steering committee made up of Jane and numerous civic and religious leaders in the county organized and met several times with the purpose of establishing a Hospice in Caldwell County.

First they had to convince the medical community of the need, as the emphasis in a physician's training in the sixties and seventies was highly technical and clinical, to fight death with all their might and to do whatever was necessary to keep a patient alive. They also understood the physicians in the community would be the key to the success of Hospice in order to refer patients. The steering committee recruited Dr. Robert Belk to become a member to encourage other physicians to understand the value of providing care for patients and their families coping with limited life expectancy. Once the planning was underway Jane preferred not to be in the limelight, but in the shadows, working in the background, believing in Hospice but encouraging others to take the lead. She was not a member of the board beyond the steering committee. The board established itself as a non-profit organization with an initial thousand dollars donated by First Presbyterian, matched by another thousand from the Lenoir Service League, and additional donations from the Episcopal Diocese. Fund raising was underway. Two years after that meeting at Jane's home, Hospice opened on June 1, 1982 with a desk, a phone, and nurse coordinator Gibbie Harris in a borrowed Sunday School classroom at First Presbyterian Church. On Sundays the desk and phone were moved to the corner of the room.

Hospice care was provided to thirty-seven families the first year. Nurses went into the homes to provide support and medical assistance. In the first edition of the organization's newsletter, Gibbie Harris explained Caldwell County's organization, "Hospice is an idea – a concept – more than it is a place. Helping the terminally ill to live – and to live well – that is what Hospice is all about."

Yet place did matter, as they were soon to discover. A block away from the makeshift Sunday School office was a most remarkable place, Kirkwood, the elegant antebellum home of Miss Margaret Harper. The front columns of the house towered above the town, dominating the landscape. The sweeping front yard ran adjacent to Church Street that led to the town. The side doors and balcony faced a carriage house where generations of young ladies once stepped onto cobblestones from horse-drawn carriages or model T Fords.

Kirkwood was built in 1840 and in its early years served as a boarding school, first for the Montrose Academy and later for the Kirkwood School for Girls with headmaster, Rev. Jesse Rankin, the minister of First Presbyterian Church. His family moved into

Kirkwood and were living there when Union troops occupied Lenoir in April, 1865. Several Confederate soldiers kept vigil from its top floor windows. Injured soldiers were cared for in the home, unaware the family treasure was hidden near them beneath the floorboards.

Two unmarried Rankin daughters continued running the school for many years until they sold the house to their brother-in-law, G. W. F. Harper, son of a prominent Lenoir family. He deeded Kirkwood in 1896 to his son, George Finley Harper. His unmarried daughter, Margaret, eventually inherited the house.

Margaret Harper died November 8, 1984 and bequeathed her family home to First Presbyterian Church specifically to be used as a Hospice facility. In a long-term, ninety-nine year agreement, the church leased the building to Hospice at the cost of one dollar per year. Months of reconstruction and preparation followed until the patient care unit opened and the first patient was admitted in February, 1989. At that time, Kirkwood was the only North Carolina inpatient Hospice facility completely independent of a hospital.

Kirkwood Hospice

The formal furnishings of the home offered a calming dimension of comfort to the patients and their families. Dr. Carswell became a fixture at Kirkwood, caring for her patients, but also often gifting them with a rose from her garden. Jane could be considered not only one of the last cradle-to-grave doctors in the county offering comprehensive care to patients of all ages, but in a twist of words, one of the very few "delivery-to-Hospice" doctors.

The overwhelming majority of end-of-life clients continued to remain in their own homes with Hospice providing support or short term respite care. Hospice staff developed a wide variety of programs targeting specific needs, counseling patients and families, or grief camps for children who lost family members. In 2005 Caldwell

Hospice added Palliative Care for those patients living with serious chronic illnesses.

In 2009 Jane attended a "Bless This House – Building on a Foundation of Prayer" service held on the site of a second facility under construction. The Jack and Shirley Robbins Center opened the following year in August of 2010. Located outside the nearby community of Hudson, it was designed with columns reminiscent of Kirkwood. Once it was in operation, the original site at Kirkwood was renovated and reopened to again serve clients.

Currently the two facilities can house a total of eighteen patients, six licensed as residential care and twelve as acute care including respite care for up to five days. The in-house patients, however, make up the smallest segment of Hospice. Ninety-four percent of care provided is in the home, as end-of-life patients most often prefer to remain in their own homes. Chief Executive Director, Cathy Swanson, reports that fifty percent of all deaths in the county in 2017 were served by Hospice. Caldwell Hospice and Palliative Care has grown to one hundred thirty-four paid staff including not only those in support positions and those in the medical field, but also four full time chaplains. Yearly operating costs amount to thirteen million dollars, funded mostly through Medicare, although Medicaid and private insurances also cover the cost of care. Support from the community through memorial gifts and contributions enable Hospice to offer enhanced services that far exceed Medicare requirements and to provide care to everyone regardless of ability to pay. The last fundraiser Hospice held was in 2009.

Jane's influence at Hospice was best summed up by her minister at that time,

> Dr. Carswell was a guiding light to Hospice of Caldwell County. With quiet determination she brought the organizing group together in the living room of her home. A Christian who blends personal piety and professional practice into a way of life, Jane Carswell makes compassion contagious. How could we turn Jane down?
>
> **Parker Williamson, Volume 1, Issue 1 Hospice Newsletter**
> **May, 1982**

Part III

FRIEND

14

Friendship

"With some folks I like to roam.
With some I like to stay home."
From an undated poem by Jane Carswell Roberts

 The world outside Lenoir, North Carolina knew Dr. Jane Carswell as the distinguished 1984 National Family Physician of the Year. The local community knew her as the doctor who would fight for her patients and their causes. But her personal friends, the ones that knew her best, knew her as a loyal companion who mixed integrity and humor with a grand sense of adventure.

They also knew her as a preeminent rose gardener with a passion for roses, whether she strolled with friends past the many bushes along the driveway to her home or appeared at their doors with freshly cut pink gifts in her hands. Her friend Nancy Gwyn was her mentor for roses, but she developed her own successful secrets, feeding the rose bushes with a variety of concoctions involving scoops of Epsom salts, cotton seed meal, bone meal and blood meal.

This passion for flowers went beyond the yellows, pinks, deep reds and whites of her roses. She sought out wildflowers and prided herself in finding a new specimen to add to the long list of native plants she photographed. A hike with Jane took hours as she identified each individual flower along the way, and instructed those along with her on its common name, its scientific name, and any local lore that was associated with it. Hiking with her was not "power walking" to arrive

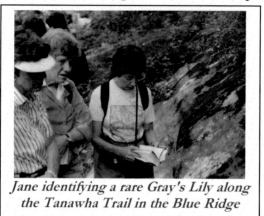

Jane identifying a rare Gray's Lily along the Tanawha Trail in the Blue Ridge

quickly at the given destination. Instead, her fellow hikers found the adventure was the trail itself with its unfolding habitat capturing their attention and time. Wednesday afternoon (her day off) often found Jane with friends scrambling over rocks telling them, "Oh, I've never seen one of those before. I'm so glad I got to see it."

As a fund raiser for the shelter home one year, Jane auctioned off a picnic hike to Gragg Prong in the Wilson Creek watershed. Dr. Marjorie Strawn was highest bidder and brought her son Matthew with her on the hike with Jane, Ken Roberts and Carol McDade. Jane prepared the picnic lunch which they ate on the rocks beside the water.

Bobbie Triplett Curtis, a county nurse, actress, and friend of Jane's, tells about a camping adventure led by Jane and Ruthie Foster to a falls, "a projected stone façade with footage to pass over on a narrow high cliff with a prayer and held breath." They backpacked in, carrying their personal items as well as their food, tarps, bedding and Bunsen burners. They arrived at the shelter on the ledge, "grilled pork chops, cinnamon covered apple slices, corn on the cob, relieved ourselves out there in the wild and slept a peaceful comfortable night. Because Jane was in our midst, we felt secure."

Another adventure with Bobbie started at a rented house in Montreat, North Carolina when Jane, who was a "fearless leader, led a few of the group on a Suicide Trail hike while others walked the Chicken Trail."

Her friend Wini remarked about hiking with Jane, "She and I would hike at places where I don't see how we ever got out of!" Jane also spent an adventurous tent camping week in Nova Scotia with another friend, Shirley Storie.

Her nephew Robert Carswell writes about spending a week each year with the entire family at the beach or a mountain retreat with Jane planning the activities and meals,

These weeks with Jane were also filled with a lot of hiking. She took us on trails all along the Blue Ridge Parkway, Appalachian Trail, and Grandfather Mountain. Jane had a great love of these mountains and an incredible ability to remember so many of its plants and trees. She was patient with our complaints and understood a teenager might need a little time to build that same appreciation. She also had no hesitations about going anywhere in those mountains. She would drive on some of the most treacherous roads and hike in terrain that was even more rugged without hesitation. On one occasion when I was around seventeen years old, we got lost (the only time I can remember that happening with Jane) on a hiking trail and ended up in the back of some old cement block shacks. It looked very unsafe. My brother and I did not think it was a good idea to approach, but Jane saw no harm in knocking on the door and asking for directions. Three women answered the door, all in hair curlers (a little outdated even in the 1980's when this took place) and Jane struck up quite a conversation with them. They turned out to be quite friendly and helpful. We never did figure out why they were getting so dressed up way up in the hills, but it taught me a lot about how our inhibitions keep us from engaging people and situations. Jane was fearless. Fearless in the sense, "why not" was asked and acted upon before excuses could be made. The "how" was never constrained by personal risk or effort when the cause was just.

When Jane arrived in Lenoir in the early sixties, her first friends and adventure companions were Nancy Gwyn and Wini Harding. One of  the activities Jane enjoyed with them was a league at the bowling alley near Jane's apartment. They became so involved with the sport they later traveled to minor tournaments throughout the western half of the state. They celebrated each other's birthdays in a wide variety of activities picked by the birthday girl. One year Wini planned for them to attend an ice hockey game, and they became ice hockey fans. Another time, they roller skated. Once.

Jane's love of sport extended into tennis, canoeing, bicycling, and in winter, cross country skiing. She and a group of friends who jokingly called themselves the "Southern Mafia," traveled often to Vermont for a winter break of exercise and conversation. One year they traveled as far as Canada to find enough snow for their cross country skiing adventure.

New York City was not the great outdoors that Jane preferred, but it was often the destination for more adventures, even beyond the quick trip to the NBC building and her television interview. Her first trip there had been a gift from her family after her college graduation. While she was walking on the street with her sister, Mary Thomas, she was fortunate to have a chance encounter (and be photographed by her sister) with Eleanor Roosevelt.

Another New York City connection with a person of note happened on an outing with Bobbie Curtis to a performance by the Philadelphia Philharmonic Orchestra at Lincoln Center. She and Bobbie were visiting Jane's former short-term intern and personal friend, Rita Redberg. After the concert, principal oboist, Lenoir native Joe Robinson, greeted Jane. His mother was one of her patients.

Bobbie described Jane at an opera production they later attended: "She wore a floor-length taffeta skirt, a colorful blouse, and had a rose pinned at her waist and one in her hair." The next evening, after a meal atop the Twin Towers, they attended a cabaret where the entertainer dragged Jane on stage to model his rendition of the theme for the night, "She's Got the Cutest Personality."

For the first few years she was in Lenoir, Jane was tied to her practice with little chance to travel for extended periods. When more physicians joined the rotation to cover evenings and weekends, she called Franke Bell, her Chapel Hill roommate. "I'm finally going to get a vacation. Let's go somewhere."

Franke had a suggestion. "I'm just getting ready to go to the Olympics in Mexico. Do you want to go?"

Franke, a swim coach in Charlotte (and a later inductee into the Swimming Coach International Hall of Fame), was attending the 1968 Olympics as a member of the press for *Swimming World Magazine*. She arranged for Jane to travel on the press charter flight and to room with a diving coach's wife outside the Olympic Village. Jane attended a variety of events, purchasing tickets at the door. Franke reports, "The thing that blew her mind, she went to the diving competitions, and back then, the Russians had to win. Their country had to win. The Russian girl in diving got second place and Jane was appalled because they took her straight out to the airport and sent her back home to Russia. They would not allow her to go to the dorm and get her clothes or anything. Jane was all upset."

On an off day, Franke accompanied Jane to a museum featuring the history of Mexico. They planned for a short visit, but stayed all day, ate lunch there, and at closing time were ushered out the door.

That small museum in Mexico City was not the only one that captivated Jane's attention in her many travels abroad. She relished finding attractions off the beaten path, even though as a tourist she dutifully, and cheerfully, walked through the grand locations of Europe. But her trip to a quaint museum in Africa was the story she enjoyed telling over and over.

She, her sister Jill, and friend Wini spent time in Rabat, Morocco while Jane was there with the Mecklenburg Medical Society. Jane attended lectures and helped with training each day, but in her free time, the three of them explored. They heard that King Hassan would be attending services at the mosque near the hotel on one particular day. Jane and Wini planned to stand outside to catch a glimpse of the king and his procession, however, they did not plan for the drenching rain that poured over them. A car pulled up and the driver motioned to them. As Wini remembers, "Jane and I looked at each other and one of us said, 'Well, there's two of us. Let's go.' We got in the car. The driver said something and we said, 'Rabat Hilton.' He nodded his head and off we went. The doorman at the hotel came running down the stairs when we arrived at the front entrance, bowing and bowing and bowing. He opened up the door and ushered us up the steps. We found out this was the chief security guard of King Hassan. The whole staff treated us like queens the rest of the time we were there."

From Morocco, they flew to Nairobi, Kenya where the mission team went into hospitals and attended classes about medical care in Kenya. Like before, in her free time, the three of them explored. They went on safari, lugging Jane's camera, waiting for the perfect shot. There in Nairobi Jane had a chance to go to the small museum that she talked about for years to come. Wini laughs about the experience saying, "When we went in, there was a little shriveled up man, the curator. He knew enough English to know that we didn't know enough of whatever he spoke, so he would go into a room, and flip the light on and stand there at the door while we would look around. Then we'd go to the next area, and he'd flip off that light and turn on the next." That was Jane's kind of museum.

Jane wrote memories of the trip in a 2009 Christmas letter to Jill. "I still have the beautiful, carved wooden rhinoceros which you bought the day we left Kenya and carried wrapped up in your raincoat all the way back to Providence Forge. Let me know when you want it back. It's living on the sun porch with other carved animals." For Christmas the following year she honored each of her brothers and sisters by funding a camel for the Maasai tribe in Africa in recognition of Jill and her fond memories of the trip to Kenya.

Jane had been to the Easter Islands and on several other trips with Elderhostel groups, so when the opportunity arose, she suggested to Wini that they travel with this same organization to the Galapagos Islands. The tour started in Quito, Ecuador where Jane had a picture taken of them standing on the equator with one foot in each hemisphere. They went on a side tour higher into the Andes Mountains where sidewalk vendors sold snacks of what Jane called, "salmonella on the foot." They ate none of that. They flew to the islands and transferred to a yacht, Jane selecting the upper bunk of their six by seven foot "stateroom" quarters. Each day opened to a new island with different animals.

Penguins lived on one island. Frigate birds and blue footed bookies were nesting on another, yet no one could disturb them to check for eggs and chicks. There were sea lions and seals and walruses with nursing babies watched over by the large bull growling at other large bulls. Jane climbed through a lava tunnel. She went snorkeling. She took pictures. Hiking the Galapagos Islands, however, was not quite the same as Jane's usual hike through the Blue Ridge Mountains since she was restricted and could not leave the path to examine a new discovery.

Jane's brother Arthur was another travel companion. With him she went to Machu Picchu and Lima, Peru on one trip and Australia and New Zealand on another. She wrote him later, "I'm sorry that I didn't know how to 'double clutch' (and still don't) and gave you some anxious moments driving down a mountain in New Zealand. I appreciated your driving the camper the rest of our stay."

Dr. Jane Carswell, family physician, humanitarian and friend lived life to the fullest. By the time she was beyond sixty-five years old, she was thinking of her future. She still had plans in mind to build that small house near her sister in Virginia and move there.

Things changed and that didn't happen.

1978 Ecuador

1978 Machu Pichu, Peru

1986 China

1995 Greece

1997 Switzerland

1997 Switzerland

15

Joy

**"To share my life is my request
With you because I love you best."**
From an undated poem by Jane Carswell Roberts

 Looking to the west from Lenoir, Jane could pick out the shape of a mountain in the distance, tracing it from a furrowed brow, down the bridge of a nose, to a beard. The first pioneers in western North Carolina named it Grandfather Mountain for the perfect silhouette of a man, an old grandfather perhaps, laying on his back. Jane knew the mountain from many angles as she hiked the trails around it and across the top of it. It presented one view from the east, and another from the west. Each season around Grandfather opened fresh perspectives to her. She camped there one winter…in the snow.

So when her friend, Suggie Styres, sometime in the early nineties mentioned a cabin on the market on the opposite side of Grandfather Mountain, Jane was intrigued. She toured it. She marveled at its deck that circled the front and part of one side, and at its kitchen window view of the back side of the Grandfather. It was just the right distance from home, far enough to escape from the constant demands of a profession, yet near enough for a quick drive up. It was just the right size, one bedroom, one bath, yet plenty of space for her nephews to unroll sleeping bags in front of the fireplace on their visits with Aunt Jane. She bought the cabin.

Grandfather Mountain as seen from Jane's cabin

In no time Jane had walked every inch and corner of her new retreat with camera in hand, always on the ready to capture the latest surprise. She identified every shrub and tree and all the wildflowers that grew so abundantly in their shade. As a bonus, her friends Suggie and Bob Styres owned the cabin next door that shared a driveway with Jane's. On the occasions when they were in the mountains at the same time, they enjoyed relaxing together, exchanging meals and examining the pictures Jane shared with them.

Since Suggie was friends with several other people who were also interested in photographing wildflowers, she invited them to come to her cabin with Jane for an evening of sharing pictures and experiences. Their friend from church, Becky Stevens, brought her photographs as did Dr. Harry Hickman, a Lenoir pediatrician who was the more advanced photographer of the group. Also present with his collection was Kenneth Roberts, the recently retired superintendent of Caldwell County Schools, who brought photographs he had taken of the many wildflowers around his home in the Happy Valley section of Caldwell County. Jane knew him by name only, although she had provided medical care to his former wife in the years prior to her death.

Jane's portfolio included pictures of two flowers Ken had seen only in photographs, but never in person. He asked where she found them, and she offered to show him. He took her up on the offer, and they made plans

Wild Geranium

White Fringed Phacelia

to meet the next day. They photographed the flowers and talked about other locations with wildflowers that they both had seen on hikes in the area, and they made specific plans to go on a photography hike.

The two of them began attending camera club meetings together and developed a mutual appreciation of each other's company that eventually blossomed into a courtship and romance. Ken accompanied her to Sunday morning worship services at her church, First Presbyterian, where they began attending holiday and special services. When Ken's daughter and son-in-law Linda and David Fisher planned a vacation to Jackson Hole, Wyoming in the spring of 1999, they invited Ken to accompany them. He and Jane had been dating, and he asked if she could come as well. The Fishers rented a three bedroom condo to serve as a base for their ten days of hiking and photography expeditions in the Tetons and in Yellowstone National Park.

As Jane and Ken became more of a couple, gentle rumors and questioning whispers began to follow them. When friends asked if there was an engagement in the future, Jane answered, "Well, that's just not so," and then added with a laugh, "There has been no question and no conversation."

The question finally did come.

In Ken's words, "I just fell in love with her, and she looked at me the same way. I bought a ring. It was Christmas 1999. We went out to eat, went back over to her house and I proposed to her."

She said, "No."

Her bewildered and scrambled explanation followed. She was set in her ways, after all she was nearly sixty-eight years old. She wanted to be free to do what she wanted to do when she wanted to do it. She would not make a good wife.

She was firm.

Ken was stunned.

An awkward gift exchange followed, and Ken went home. Jane left town the next day to spend the Christmas holidays with her family at her sister Judy's home in Lumberton.

For two weeks Jane and Ken had no communication. His mind went over and over what had happened. "Maybe we ought to have talked some. I could have handled it better, but she was so definite. If she had said 'Let's think about it,' it might have been different."

Her mind also went over and over what had happened. She talked with her sister about the possibilities. She confided in a few friends.

She made a decision, returned to Lenoir, and called Ken. "We need to talk." She immediately came to his house.

He had no idea what she was going to say to him. She had no idea what he would say to her.

"Do you still want me to marry you?" she asked.

"Of course. Will you?"

This time she said, "Yes!"

Jane pulled her mother's engagement ring from her coat pocket, the very ring that her father had bought in haste when her mother came to him all those years ago, warning him he needed to leave town. "Do you mind if I wear this for an engagement ring?"

But Ken just happened to already have one. She had not seen it, since he had had no chance to show it to her at his proposal. The "No" had come too fast. He had not returned it, though, but kept it in a back closet.

She put away her mother's ring and accepted Ken's. She tried it on, but it was a fraction too large. "I'll get it sized," she promised.

He asked her about setting a date. She responded, "I don't believe in long engagements. It takes a while to plan a wedding, so I need to get started."

What began as an awkward encounter turned into relief and unexpected happiness. They made plans to drive to the mountains the following evening for dinner to celebrate.

The next morning, though, she went to a church meeting at the Catholic Center in nearby Hickory, and for the first time, wore her ring in public. Her engagement created quite a stir, as her thrilled friends admired the ring and congratulated her.

After lunch she privately looked down to marvel at her ring once again, but it wasn't there. She immediately realized that it had slipped off her finger. She panicked and announced in her loudest voice possible, "Stay where you are!" Everyone began a search for the ring, but they could not locate it. Jane remembered that she had taken her paper plates to the garbage can, so she dug through the trash. Others joined in, and after much anguish at the task they were attempting, they found it.

By the time Jane arrived at Ken's door that evening for their celebration trip to the mountains, "She was a different person, just glowing with happiness and excitement." Her voice quivered when she told him she almost lost the ring.

They set the wedding date, May 20, 2000. Her roses would be in bloom by then, and so would other flowers that she loved so well. Becky Stevens offered to decorate with mountain laurel from Ken's place and with roses gathered from both Jane's and her friend Nancy Gwyn's yards. Jane selected a light pink dress to wear. A location was chosen, First Presbyterian with the minister, Rev. Gerritt Dawson, and Jane's sister Jill's husband, Rev. Hal Wallof, both officiating. A reception would follow in the fellowship hall. Ken's family, including his three children, Ken, Jr., Steve, and Linda, along with his sixteen year old grandson, Dustin, would be there to support him. Jane's family, including her nephews, David, Jay, Scott and Robert, would be there to support her. Invitations went out to their friends and family.

The day of the ceremony, guests arrived from as far away as Guatemala, Virginia, California and all corners of North Carolina. They watched as Jane entered unescorted from the side door to meet Ken at the altar. When the minister came to the part in the service where he asked, "Who giveth this woman?" they witnessed her entire family stand and proudly proclaim, "We do!"

For their honeymoon, they chose a location in the mountains within a short drive after the wedding, the Peaks of Otter, off the Blue Ridge Parkway in Virginia where they could hike and enjoy the flowers. That particular year, the mountain laurel and purple rhododendron proved to be spectacular. Each trail they hiked seemed to offer more clusters of blooms than the last. The following year the couple returned on the same date. The weather was rainy and cold, and as Ken remembers, there was not a bloom in sight. Each anniversary from then on, they spent three days somewhere in the mountains.

Ken asked where she preferred to live, his home or her home, or if she would want them to build or purchase a new home. "Yours," she said. His had woods. His had wild flowers. His was on a hill overlooking Happy Valley, with the Yadkin River in the distance. The decision was not hard for her to make. Several months after the wedding she sold her house.

The one thing his house did not have was her rose bushes, and she was determined to transplant them, all thirty-seven of them, as they had planned to do before the wedding. Her family discouraged her, even offering money to purchase new ones so she would not be overwhelmed by the necessary labor. She was sixty-eight years old, they reminded her, and her new husband, sixty-six. They gifted her with ten new rose bushes and Ken set them out for her in a small circle in the front yard.

But Jane missed her own roses, the ones she had nurtured and fed and pruned and coaxed into beauty. She could not leave them behind. She and Ken researched how to transplant these huge bushes and keep them healthy in their new plots. Each bush would require a hole eighteen inches  in diameter and eighteen inches deep. Heavy soil would need to be moved along with the plants. The task appeared daunting, but still they were determined.

They plotted where each rose bush would eventually go and killed off any surrounding grass. They investigated a gasoline operated machine to dig the holes, but realized it was more than they cared to handle. Ken experimented on his own to find how hard digging the holes would be. Fortunately the condition of the soil was perfect for shoveling, neither too wet nor too dry. He used a mattock to dig the first hole, then the second, and then as many as he could before dark. The next day they went to Jane's house where Ken found that digging the bushes there was even easier than preparing the holes that were waiting for them. Jane helped transfer the bushes into plastic bags retaining as much of the dirt from around the roots as possible. She worked alongside him, helping with the loading and planting. They moved a pickup truckload at a time, and over a twenty-four hour period, Jane's rose bushes were in their new location. One bush, however,  did not survive, and Jane performed an autopsy on it only to discover that in their digging, they had accidentally severed its main root.

Jane and Ken soon settled into a routine. For professional reasons, she did not change her legal name, but socially she became known as Jane Roberts. She fretted that Ken would tire of the same meal, and she experimented with new recipes, although according to him, she knew how to warm left overs to make them almost new. She admitted to him that she learned about left overs, because once in her early single years, she and two other friends decided to swap their left overs to add a little variety to their daily meals.

Ken typically prepared breakfast, so it was usually cereal, fruit and coffee although on special occasions for the two of them or when they had overnight company, he prepared a full meal with bacon, eggs, pancakes, and fruit. On Sunday mornings after breakfast, Jane started cooking, setting the food in the oven with a timer so lunch would be ready when they arrived home from church. Her hospitality was well known throughout the community. Their friend, Dianne Hubbard, writes, "She always provided a gracious welcome for visitors, and her cooking deserved to be as legendary as her medical work - with classic Southern food that often featured homegrown produce."

Jane wrote in her Christmas letter one year about that homegrown produce, "Our garden kept us busy, and we are enjoying the frozen corn, peas, butter beans, and other vegetables now. We also enjoyed making pickles and fig preserves." In another Christmas letter she wrote, "Living on the edge of the woods is great, but also involves visits from deer, rabbits, turkeys, raccoons, possums, dozens of squirrels, and other varmints who also enjoy the fruits of our labors." She claimed there were tomato devouring deer and green bean addicted groundhogs living in their woods.

During her medical career Jane had been the physician who had the time, the energy, and the passion to devote to a variety of humanitarian causes, while her friends and colleagues devoted their time, energies and passions to raising a family. They volunteered to help Jane whenever their busy schedules allowed. Now Jane found the joy they already knew, but had not been a part of her life. She relished having family, children and grandchildren that she lovingly referred to as "ours," not "his."

In 2003, Ken's daughter Linda and her husband David adopted their first child, John. Ken and Jane met them at their house when they returned from Utah with the baby and helped them settle in with a

Jane with John and holding Daniel

newborn. In fact, Jane took care of the baby the first night home so the weary parents could sleep. They adopted a second child, Daniel, in 2005 and due to the nature of the adoption process, left eighteen-month old John with Ken and Jane for ten days. Linda wrote in a letter about the experience,

It was so difficult for us, but Dad and Jane took him everywhere and took great care of him. We sent Dad a picture of Daniel as soon as we had one, and Dad would show it to John and talk about his brother. It was heartbreaking to be away from John during that time, but it was made easier knowing that he was so loved and so well-cared for at their home. Our children had an instant bond with them...She loved our boys and she loved spending time with them. When they were young, she would always get down in the floor and play with them. She had a way of teaching as she played and our children learned a lot from her. Both Jane and Dad loved teaching our children about nature and our children love them dearly.

When Ken was helping David build a playhouse at their home one year, Daniel, the younger of the two, was especially fascinated with all the nuts, bolts, and screws. He wanted to play with them, and Jane's job was to keep him away from the "million" parts that the structure came in. Meanwhile, John, the older brother, loved to "help," and aided Jane in her cookie making by pouring a half box of salt in the dough.

Having a built-in medical advisor in the family came as a bonus to the young mother who relied on Jane's recommendations. Likewise, Ken's son Steve and his wife Meagan learned to rely on Jane's wisdom as they raised their two children. Their daughter Celia was born in 2009. Since they lived next door and only a brief walk away, Jane became Celia's best buddy. Jane crawled on the floor with her as she had with John and Daniel. Jane's love of butterbeans turned into a sharing time with Celia as they hulled the beans together and stocked the freezer for a year's supply. They

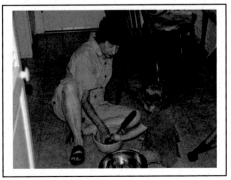

played with the Happy Hands puppets and assumed the characters, often remaining in their roles beyond playtime. Their favorite game was "school" – Celia as teacher, Jane and Rufus, the puppet, as students. Jane often had Rufus misbehave, and Celia would respond, "Rufus, if you do that one more time!"

Celia remembers quite a bit of her time with Jane, even though she was only a kindergartner when Jane died in 2015. She remembers the piano keyboard Jane played for her and she can still play the one song Jane taught her. Her younger brother Samuel was only a few months old and has no personal memory of Jane.

Their oldest grandson, Dustin, who was sixteen years old at their wedding, visited during the Christmas season each year. Although he lived out of state, he had a good relationship with Jane. His two daughters, Ashlyn and Brooklyn, made Jane and Ken great-grandparents and added two more delightful children to Christmas celebrations.

Ever the poet, Jane often wrote short verses that she scattered around the house for Ken to discover. One in particular found its way into his heart, and his billfold, where it remains today. It was a typed note, but she had signed it in her own script.

With some folks I like to roam.
With some I like to stay home.
Some are great to share our joys.
With some we like to share our toys.
Some may go with us to ski?
And some go on a wildflower spree.
Of all the folks I know it's you
Who fits the bill best thru and thru.
To share my life is my request
With you because I love you best.

Love always,

Jane

16

Retirement

"We are both feeling fine and are active in a variety of things which are so diverse that sometimes we feel like several different people."
Jane Carswell Roberts in her 2006 Christmas letter to friends

 Combining two households meant Jane and Ken needed to decide which relics from their former lives would stay and which would be eliminated. Besides the rose bushes, Jane transplanted many of her beloved flower bulbs and plants. That was for the outside where there was ample room for extras. Inside was a different story. She could not part with the plaques and awards and newspaper articles about her, not because she wanted to bask in glory, but because she felt truly honored by each thoughtful recognition. Neither could she part with the myriad of photographs she had taken over the years and stored in scrapbooks.

And then, there were the Christmas ornaments. Although the climax at every Christmas for Jane was the Interracial Program, she had developed a number of traditions on her own. For many years, she invited personal friends to her home to help decorate her Christmas tree. She had purchased none of her own ornaments, and yet the tree itself was covered. She knew each decoration hanging on the tree and told her friends where it had come from, who had given it to her, and when she had received it. She brought these ornaments with her, only now she told the stories to her new family. Ken's daughter, Linda, writes of Christmas with Jane:

At Christmas, their house was always adorned with numerous interesting decorations with lots of history for Jane. She loved showing them to the children and telling how she acquired them. They especially loved watching and listening to her many music boxes. Jane always made Christmas such a special celebration.

Jane shared more than decorations. She shared her cabin in the mountains. Her own nephews had grown beyond overnights with Aunt Jane, so now she and Ken began the overnights with their grandchildren. According to Linda,

When our children were old enough, Dad and Jane started a tradition that we always called 'Camp Grandma and Grandpa.' They would take the children to the mountains for most of a week during the summer. With the exception of their last trip, they stayed at Jane's cabin at Seven Devils. Dad and Jane would take them fishing, gem mining, hiking, and all sorts of other activities. On the last trip, Dad and Jane took them to Cherokee because Daniel was studying a lot about that in school.

I recently asked my children about their fondest memories of Jane. They both immediately mentioned the trips to Jane's cabin. They loved spending time with her there. Though simple, they loved that cabin. Jane had many wooden 'mountain toys' and the children loved playing with her with these. Although Dad and Jane were always involved in many things, when John and Daniel were visiting, they were entirely focused on them. I think the cabin represents all the love that my children felt from Jane – and from my father. Dad and Jane also introduced them to Price's Park, and this became one of their favorite activities. They loved playing in the stream there and often found other children to play with as well. Before going there the first time, they were hesitant to go because they thought they would be bored. Dad and Jane got them interested in nature and taught them a lot.

Looking Glass Falls near Brevard

Hiking both with and without the grandchildren continued to be a passion for Ken and Jane. Although they roamed throughout the Blue Ridge Mountains and well beyond, one of their favorite destinations was much closer, Wilson Creek, a section in western Caldwell County that in 2000, had been designated as a nationally protected Wild and Scenic River. After the Wilson Creek Visitor Center opened in 2002, Jane and Ken joined The Friends of Wilson Creek, a volunteer group of concerned environmentalists.

One project Jane undertook at the center was a wildflower identification display. Often visitors came into the center asking about a particular flower that Jane could easily identify if she had been present. She had taken numerous photographs of flowers in the area, so she printed copies of each of the flowers and then prepared individual pages to include interesting pertinent scientific information. One volunteer, Homer Gragg, designed a weatherized box to hold an oversized rolodex containing these identification cards. It was placed at the wildflower garden adjacent to the visitor center.

The wildflower identification box

This garden was another project that Jane passionately supported. She and Ken and board member Susan Powers were distressed to find the land alongside the creek at the center had been scraped and graded clean, with no growth to shade the water and maintain the cool natural temperatures that were necessary for the overall health of the stream system. They began tending the patch of stream that led beside the center to the main Wilson Creek channel. They researched native plants that contributed to preserving the eco-system and then transplanted species that within a few years restored the stream to a more natural habitat. They fought to remove nonnative plants, especially Japanese knotweed, long considered a scourge worse than kudzu to the undergrowth of the forests. It had been planted years before, higher in the mountains, but seeds had floated downstream and established outgrowths along the banks. They were proud to show their work when they hosted a meeting of the North Carolina Native

Plant Society in 2013. They scouted out trail possibilities and led the members on hikes.

The trail beside the visitor's center

When a corporation applied to build over two hundred cabins along the creek, Jane sounded alarm against overdevelopment. She made many phone calls. She appeared before the county commissioners, and in the end, the company eventually withdrew its plan.

The mission of the wild and scenic river designation was not only to protect the natural beauty of the area, but also to preserve its history and culture. Jane was chairman of the program committee that organized monthly activities ranging from discovery walks for children, to historical hikes through the ruins of an old cotton mill, to afternoon events with long established families who lived in the area. She set out to learn about the history of communities along the creek and she interviewed the family members of the early settlers. She wrote a script featuring noted furniture maker, Bill Crump, and then organized Bill Crump Day. She found people that owned pieces of his furniture he had made almost a century before. That day, they brought a total of nineteen small pieces and several photographs showing many examples of his larger furniture to put on display.

Jane's discovery on a hike to the Bill Crump place

One day Jane and Ken were hiking with her nephew, David Carswell, showing him their favorite stream in the Wilson Creek watershed, when they stopped to rest at the foot of the Gragg Prong waterfalls. They noticed several rather large trout in the small pool, and they saw a snake swim nearby, but thought the fish were too large for it to bother. Suddenly David said, "That snake has caught a fish!"

The snake, a northern water snake, fought with the fish for a long time before Jane remembered the point-and-shoot camera in her backpack. She missed taking shots of the initial battle as it gained complete control of the fish, but she did capture the final scenes. This series of photographs hangs in the Wilson Creek Visitor's Center on display with several others Jane shot. It shows the progression of the snake eating the fish and is considered the favorite display at the center.

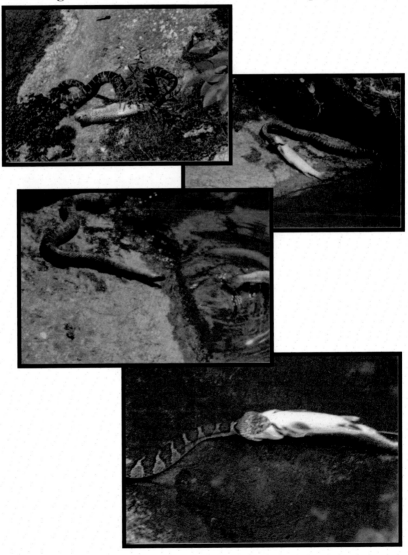

Before it was destroyed by fire, Jane had walked through the once elegant Edgemont Hotel that was a summer train ride destination for flatland tourists seeking the coolness of the mountains in the days before air conditioning. She saw the effects of the devastating hurricanes and ensuing floods of 1916 and 1940 that destroyed all economic progress and contributed in their own way to keeping Wilson Creek wild and scenic. She explored the Mortimer Civilian Conservation Corps site where she saw the impact that depression era program made to the area. She learned about the lumber companies of the early twentieth century who timbered the mountainside, and about how they built a railroad into the area to ship the logs out. She knocked on the door of the former Edgemont Depot, built in 1906 and by then in use as a private lodge, and was invited inside for a tour by the daughter of the current owner. She shared all she had learned as she and Ken led groups on historical hikes. She created scripts based on her research and recruited friends to portray the characters she wrote about for the 2012 self-guided tours at Wilson Creek's History Day: the clerk at the company store (Nelson Brookshire), a laborer in the cotton mill (Becky Stevens), a CCC worker (Mike Pruitt), the stationmaster at the depot (Brandon McCann), a member of Edgemont Baptist Church (Bobbie Curtis), and the actual descendants of the original 1895 Edgemont store owner (Dewayne and Virginia Pyatte). One sentence Jane wrote in the CCC script gives insight into why she was dedicated, "They say that if you ever get your feet wet in Wilson Creek, you'll never leave."

Her contributions extended beyond wildflowers and history. She was the designated medical person for children's inner tube trips down the creek. She directed another activity that pressed a leaf into clay, then baked the prints at her own home and returned them the next week. She combined her love of hiking with her love of photography and organized a photography contest, realizing the publicity would not only interest others in Wilson Creek, but would showcase its beauty as well.

The idea was simple. Make rules: Photographs must be taken during that calendar year in the Wilson Creek watershed and then framed using specific guidelines. Publicize the contest, especially with camera clubs, to attract a wide variety of entries. Find distinguished judges, like Hugh Morton, owner of Grandfather Mountain and a renowned photographer in his own right. Award cash prizes, seventy-five dollars for first prize, fifty for second, and twenty-five for third. Charge a five dollar entry fee per piece. Hold an opening reception where the winners are unveiled. Sponsor a juried exhibition for a month in the upstairs gallery at the Wilson Creek Visitor's Center.

The response was so wonderful, the contest was held for several years. Photographs arrived showing waterfalls and hillsides and mossy creek banks in all four seasons. Winners were selected. A few of the winning pictures remain hanging in the Visitor Center on permanent display.

Ken took this of Jane taking photographs on Wilson Creek.
A print of it now hangs in the new Hospice facility.

Even though she was retired and able to spend an extraordinary amount of time following the many trails through the Wilson Creek watershed of the photography contest, Jane did not give up her medical license. She wanted to be available in case she was needed at the women's shelter, or at the free clinic, or at the halfway house, or in the back woods of the Blue Ridge. She visited elderly neighbors who could not travel easily to town and offered minor treatments. A local farmer brought her a load of manure for her roses as a special thank you.

One man in particular was fortunate that she was still available and in the right place at the right time. She and Ken were returning home from Winston-Salem along a four lane highway, Ken behind the wheel. An out of control pickup truck ran off the side of the highway ahead of them, overcorrected and streamed to the other side, overcorrected again, and rolled side over side onto the shoulder and over the guard rail. Ken stopped his car, not only because they had witnessed the accident, but also because Jane was a physician who, from the beginning of her training, had vowed to respond in a medical crisis. He called for emergency help while she rushed to the man, running despite the fact she was in her late seventies. A bystander who identified himself as an off-duty first responder advised her to stop. "He's dead. There's no use." Jane would not accept that. He was not breathing, so she reached inside his mouth to dislodge his tongue and free his airway, soaking her hand in his blood. He immediately began breathing, and by the time Ken caught up with her, she had finished working with the victim. Once he was loaded inside the ambulance, the emergency technicians turned their attention to Jane and the blood on her unprotected hand.

When she arrived home, she put three pairs of surgical gloves in the car. Fortunately she never found a need to use them.

Jane remained up to date on the latest in medical breakthroughs. One way she accomplished this was through audio digest, featuring lectures made by experts on various illnesses. To keep her medical license current, she was required to earn fifty hours of continuing education, which gave Jane and Ken an excuse to travel to conferences throughout the United States. She attended a Travel and Wilderness Medicine seminar in Santa Fe, New Mexico, where she laughingly reported the most valuable information gleaned was to "take safety pins and duct tape when you venture into the backwoods." While they were there, she and Ken traveled to the cliff dwellings in Bandelier, to Las Alamos and to Ghost Ranch. She attended the national Family Practice assembly in Chicago to earn continuing education hours, and they visited museums and parks, and saw the play *Wicked*. They went to Alaska on a medical trip, but returned another year with friends on a cruise where they saw a different region of the state from their earlier visit.

They attended a Humanities Forum sponsored by Lenoir Rhyne College at a retreat in the North Carolina mountains. They went to an Elderhostel in Charlottesville, Virginia where they learned about Jefferson, Madison and Monroe. They visited a friend in Florida and enjoyed Fernandina Beach and nearby Cumberland Island. They traveled to Costa Rica with good friends Bob and Ruthie Foster. They went to Bermuda with Jane's sister and her husband, Jill and Hal Wallof. They spent two weeks in Germany with a group led by Oscar and Ingrid Dobereiner where they cruised the Rhine and visited several cities. One memorable event was on a horse-drawn wagon ride through fields of blooming heather with an accordion player and singer accompanying them. Jane stopped for a picture opportunity with a shepherd tending his flock.

Jane's chance encounter with a shepherd at work

A grand opportunity was offered to them in 2004 that proved to be the memorable experience beyond all the others. Ken's secretary when he was principal and school superintendent, Dot Hubbard, and her husband, Rudolph, the agriculture teacher where Ken was principal, remained close personal friends with him after they all retired. Their daughter, Dianne, had married and was living in Windhoek, Namibia on the African continent, and Ken had traveled there twice with them. With an ocean between Dianne and her parents, Ken and Jane were happy to spend time with the couple, almost daily after Dot suffered from a stroke. After her death, Jane and Ken maintained close contact with him. Dianne wrote about Jane, "I lived far away from my old hometown by then, and I remember with great fondness how she organized a lovely eightieth birthday party for my father, with guests gathered around a beautifully-laid table in an atmosphere of warmth and cheer."

When Dianne invited them to come to Africa and escort her father on his long trip across the Atlantic, they could not resist. Dianne and Ken prepared an itinerary for them to tour Namibia and South Africa while her father visited in her home. Jane and Ken traveled first into the Namib Desert, one of the most photogenic spots on earth. They flew in on a small private plane where they were limited to twenty-five pounds of luggage, including camera equipment. Their accommodations were in tents with finished hardwood floors and a

145

masonry bathroom attached. On the top of the bathroom was a flat roof with linens and blankets provided for them to sleep outside where, under a pollution-free sky, they had an endless view of stars. Jane wrote to a friend, "We slept on the roof one night, and the stars seemed within our grasp, especially the Milky Way."

Awards Won
Slide of the Year – Catawba Valley Camera Club
Best in Show – Caldwell County Arts Council
Photo Contest

The next morning as they traveled by land rover across the desert floor, she took an award winning photograph that captured the colors of the towering thousand foot high red sand dunes surrounding them.

They flew next from Wolwedans to Swakopmund where their accommodations were at an elegant four star hotel. Their room was "as big as the first floor of my house," Ken claims, "two baths, a full kitchen, full dining room, and thirteen closets." Because they had been limited in what luggage they could bring, they had packed minimal clothing and were not prepared for elegant dining, especially after they were driven by land rover to an old whaling station that had been covered by drifting sand. They ordered room service.

They traveled by overnight train back to Dianne's home to spend time visiting before Dianne and her husband Andrew Corbett, and their children hosted them on a three day safari to Etosha National Park. Their group was in the game park and lingered a little too long watching a lion eating an elephant, and then even longer watching a pride of lions. When they returned to the fenced enclosure where they were to sleep, it had been locked for the night. Andrew drove his vehicle next to the gate and used it to attempt climbing over the gate to get inside one way or the other and not spend the night with the wild animals around them. A man finally opened the gate for them to pass through.

Dianne Hubbard, center, with her husband Andrew Corbett, her children and Jane at Etosha National Park

Jane and Ken left Namibia and traveled to Cape Town, South Africa to be the guests of Andrew's parents, Michael and Peggy Corbett. Although side trips to see the Cape of Good Hope, Table Mountain, and Kirstenbosch Gardens were especially enjoyable to them, their tour of Robben Island, the location where Nelson Mandela was held prisoner for eighteen years, turned out to be the experience that impressed them most. The guides there were former residents with Mandela and told stories about their time in the prison. Michael Corbett had been the chief justice who swore in Mandela to the presidency. As the two couples visited with each other, Jane and Ken enjoyed hearing about the Corbetts' experiences during South Africa's transition from apartheid. Peggy told about the election when Mandela became president, the festive atmosphere and the fact that they knew the voting lines would be so long, everyone would become hungry. Many people, both black and white, including Peggy Corbett, took food to share with those standing in line. Jane recognized the significance of her meeting this esteemed man, yet she felt just as comfortable with him as she had felt in the desert restaurant talking with the waiters about their families. Dianne wrote about her friend, "Jane was at home anywhere, because her ease and confidence and attitude of care travelled with her and made others comfortable in her presence."

This same level of ease and comfort helped Jane through a challenge she had facing her at home in Lenoir. For her entire life she had been not only a devout Christian, but also a devoted Presbyterian. She had been vocal in defending the value of all people as a response to her faith. She crusaded for the rights of the abused and battered, the uninsured, the elderly, and the teenagers. In her medical practice, she did not distinguish between ethnic backgrounds, race, religion, sexual orientation or gender. She and Ken attended worship services and supported the church in many ways, but they came to the realization that their beliefs conflicted with a stand taken by church leadership. After much prayer, soul searching, questioning interactions with others, and private conversations between them as a couple, Jane and Ken visited other congregations and then decided to move their church membership to Fairview Presbyterian Church, a much smaller congregation on the western side of town.

Once again they became immersed in church activities, and as an introduction to themselves, invited the "Young at Heart" group from Fairview to Happy Valley for an historical tour led by Ken. Jane made several presentations about her mission trips to Guatemala that encouraged others in the congregation to become involved and travel on missions. They joined in the food pantry program the church had started under the leadership of Carol Walker and Randy Helton. Jane brought her expertise in writing grant proposals and helped acquire additional funding for the pantry.

Fairview's Food Pantry began in 2002 to meet the needs of the many people in the county who came by the church asking for help. During the years when the furniture factories were closing and families were struggling with hunger, Fairview's "Pay It Forward" food bank was there to respond. In the beginning it was open from eleven to one forty-five on the second and fourth Thursdays of each month. When the need became greater, it added once a month Saturday morning distribution hours. Financial support came through grants, private donations and fundraisers, such as an auction held at the church. Food was obtained through the Second Harvest Food Bank of Northwest North Carolina. She and Ken went with others to meet the Second Harvest truck at the drop-off site on Wednesdays, to offload the food and transfer it to their own pantry on pickup truck loads, a ministry that Ken continues after Jane's death. In addition to food and used clothing, the pantry gave items that could not be purchased with EBT (Medicaid) cards. Jane explained the mission at its tenth year anniversary in 2015:

As the name Pay It Forward implies, we ask clients to try to do something to help someone else. Many volunteer to work in the Pantry. Others may just help a neighbor by furnishing a ride or doing small jobs for them. Probably most important, clients are provided a listening ear. We see each family privately and give them an opportunity to talk about their problems. They are given a list and explanation of available community resources. Sometimes contacts are made for them.

The church operated a backpack ministry in connection with the Pay it Forward Pantry sending twenty-six children from Davenport A+ Elementary School home on Fridays with food packed in specially provided backpacks. Not only did Jane write grants for funding, she also helped the Women of the Church pack the food after their monthly meetings.

When a church member bequeathed his home to the church at his death, Jane helped others clean the house to prepare temporary shelter for residents from Koinonia whose apartments were undergoing renovations. After the last resident returned to Koinonia, the house was transformed into the Pay It Forward Food Bank building.

Jane seemed to have an unending supply of energy. If there were a fellowship meal, or a bereavement meal for a family, she was there helping, and she remained afterward until the hall was cleaned. She continued dropping in at the shelter home and Helping Hands. She wrote the newsletter for Caldwell House. She maintained her medical license, but finally made the decision to give it up on her eighty-third birthday, February 26, 2015, as she wanted to spend more time with her family. She was starting to slow down, and she noticed a drop in her energy. When walking to the mailbox one day, she mentioned to Ken that she was getting out of shape, that she needed to exercise more because she was having a bit of a difficulty.

She called her personal physician, Dr. Nancy Morgan, and made an appointment for a Monday afternoon. She called Ken from the doctor's office that day, and in a calm voice said to him, "Could you come get me? Nancy said I shouldn't drive."

She called back in five minutes and again in a calm voice said to Ken, "Nancy's sending me to Frye Hospital in an ambulance."

Ken rushed to the hospital. His son Steve came shortly after, and by the time they both arrived, she was in the cardiac catheterization lab. She had had a heart attack, a relatively minor one, but she had come through surgery well and was sent to intensive care. The surgeon was pleased at how she responded, and showed Ken what they had done. "She'll be in here, maybe three days, and then go home," he said.

By Wednesday morning, she was feeling much better. The doctors released her from intensive care, but because there was no patient room available, she remained there for several more hours. She and Ken had a chance to visit with each other, to spend time talking, with few hospital interruptions. Around noon, Jane encouraged him to go home and get some rest. Ken realized she also needed to rest, said goodbye, and left for the day, assuring her that he would be there to bring her home when she would be discharged the next morning. She called him around 2:30 to say that she had been moved from intensive care to a room, that she had walked to the room, and that she felt fine. He called her around 5:30, checking in with her. Once again she said she felt fine. She answered phone calls from friends. She sat in a chair by the window, reading a book.

Ken's son, Ken Jr. was a nurse at Frye Hospital there in Hickory, and he came by, intending to speak to her that evening before he went home. As he walked through the hall he heard a code blue, and quickly realized it was for Jane. The hospital called Ken while Ken, Jr. on his own called his brother, Steve, and told him to bring their father to the hospital, that things did not look promising.

Ken walked into the hospital expecting the worst, and it was.

The doctors were stunned. They had done everything they could, yet they could not save Jane.

The date was March 25, 2015.

Ken's daughter, Linda finished her letter with these comments that speak for everyone who ever knew Jane:

Our lives were greatly enriched by Jane's presence. We are still so sad that our lives with her were cut so abruptly and so short. Jane gave so much in her life, but still had so much more to give. Jane was such a fine Christian woman that daily practiced what she believed. Her life was truly modeled after Jesus in that she was always helping those that society seemed to forget. She had a wonderful way of communicating to other people across all segments of society. Jane had a tremendous sense of right and wrong. I will always be amazed at her interest in all people that she came in contact with and her ability to stay in touch with all of them. She was an amazing woman, and we miss her dearly. My biggest regret is the time that my children lost to spend with her. I regret that they lost her before they were old enough to understand her as more than just a loving grandmother.

Months later when their granddaughter Celia was in the car as Ken picked her up after school, she said to him, "I miss Grandma more than anybody does."

After a moment of silence, Ken managed to respond. "No. I'm sorry. I miss Grandma more than anybody."

She hesitated, thought a bit and then said, "Okay. So it's a tie."

From Jane's 2010 Interracial Christmas Program Script:

Tonight, as is traditional, we will close with a candle lighting service. As you see the light of candles approaching you, think of God's great love for you. Think of His being willing to send His Son into a world of sinful people, which includes us all. Then as you light the candle of the person next to you, think of the ways that you can help show God's love to other people.

Caldwell Friends
918 West Ave. SW Suite 206
Lenoir, NC 28645
www.caldwellfriends.com

Caldwell Hospice and Palliative Care, Inc.
902 Kirkwood Street NW
Lenoir, NC 28645
www.caldwellhospice.org

Caldwell House
951 Kenham Pl SW
Lenoir, NC 28645.
www.thecaldwellhouse.com

Helping Hands Clinic of Caldwell County
810 Harper Avenue NW
Lenoir, NC 28645
www.helpinghandsclinic.org

Pay It Forward Food Pantry
Fairview Presbyterian Church
2058 Harper Avenue NW
Lenoir, NC 28645
www.fairviewpresbyterianchurch.com

Shelter Home of Caldwell County
PO Box 426
Lenoir, NC 28645
www.shelterhomecc.org

Sisters of Notre Dame
1601 Dixie Highway
Covington, Kentucky 41011
www.sndky.org

ACKNOWLEDGEMENTS

A large portion of this book comes directly from Jane Carswell's creative writings, her written recollections and personal correspondences, supplemented with additional stories from Ken Roberts.

Special appreciation and thanks to the many who contributed their own recollections of Jane and the causes that were dear to her: Linda Roberts Fisher and Robert Carswell for the family history and stories; Patsy Conoley, the Raeford Hoke Museum, Jane Davis, and the Flora Macdonald Legacy Board; Saradee Davis Bowen, Sue Jones Jessick, and Franke Bell; Sr. Joan Niklas, the Sisters of Notre Dame, Covington, Kentucky, Dwain Lester, MaryJo and Mike O'Bradovich; Wini Harding, Susan Cogdell Schilling, Mary Caroline Cogdell, Lucy McCarl, Charles Hooper, Sue Ellen and Nelson Brookshire, Lynne Plymale, Drs. Charles Scheil, Nancy Morgan, John McMenemy, Rita Redberg, and Scott Lurie; Jimmie and Mary Alice Norwood, Parker Williamson, Becky Stevens, Helen Hall and Jennie Deal; Debi Nelson, Sharon Poarch Cook, Lisa Clontz, Ruth Kincaid, and Terri Niederhammer; Bob Laws; Cathy Swanson, Susan Rudisill, Gwin Laws, and Charlie Frye; Judith Nebrig, Dr. Douglas Michael, and Virginia Stevens; Debra Philyaw, Tom Withem, and Lilly Bunch; Chastity Triplett; Bobbie Curtis, Suggie Styres, Dianne Hubbard, Lois Clark, Carol McDade, Glynis James, and Rick Rash; and many others who shared a story in passing.

And others who helped with making this book happen: *Books That Matter,* Spencer Ainsley, Guy Lucas, the Lenoir *News-Topic,* Beth Davison, Bill Tate, Doug Terry, Jan Pritchard, Jodi Smith with the Medical College of Virginia, John Craig, Barbara Watson, Cindy Day, Sandra Warren, Debbie Allmand, Teresa Fannin, and Van Griffith for his constant support.

ORGANIZATION ARCHIVES

Caldwell County Hospice and Palliative Care, Inc., Lenoir, North Carolina.
Caldwell County Shelter Home, Lenoir, North Carolina.
Caldwell Heritage Museum, Lenoir, North Carolina.
Jim McKee Local History Room, Caldwell County Public Library, Lenoir, North Carolina.
Lynch, Kentucky 100 Years Committee, Lynch, Kentucky.
Raeford Hoke Museum, Raeford, North Carolina.
Sisters of Notre Dame, Covington, Kentucky.
Western North Carolina Presbytery, Morganton, North Carolina.

ADDITIONAL SOURCES

Alexander, Nancy. A Medical History of Caldwell County. Lenoir, North Carolina: Nancy Alexander. 1981.

Blue, Malcolm. "Family Physician of Year." The Sandhills Citizen and News Outlook 12 Dec. 1984: A8

Bostian, Frank K. Dr. Margaret Caroline McNairy: Her Dreams Came True. Charlotte, North Carolina: The Delmar Co. 1980.

Denton, Van. "Dr. Carswell Named US Practitioner of on NBC." Lenoir News-Topic 4 Oct. 1984: 1, 12.

Denton, Van. "NBC to Feature Doctor Carswell in Health Series." Lenoir News-Topic 3 September 1984: 1, 10.

"Family Physician of Year forgoes Ego Boosting for Community Service." Charlotte Observer 9 Dec. 1984: B6.

"FP Fills Needs of Public, Physician." Family Practice Highlights Winter 1984: 1, 3.

Gleasner, Diana. "Dr. Jane Carswell: 1984 Family Physician of the Year." New Woman Magazine June 1985: 34.

Howard, Jane. "She has a Practice That's Almost Perfect." Family Weekly 18 Aug. 1985: 4.

"Lenoir Doctor is Honored By Peers." Lincolnton News 10 Dec. 1984: 5.

McCarl, Lucy F. You Shall Be My People: A History of the First Presbyterian Church, Lenoir, North Carolina. Greenville, South Carolina: A Press. 2002.

McCormack, Patricia. "Woman Named Family Doctor of the Year." The Weatherford (Texas) Democrat 7 Nov. 1984: 11.

Reagan, Cleve. "Dr. Carswell, Wilson Chosen Dysart Winners." Lenoir News-Topic 23 January 1980: 1, 14.

ABOUT THE AUTHOR

Gretchen Griffith is a former Caldwell County teacher with thirty years of experience covering multiple levels from Head Start five year olds to freshmen at Appalachian State University and Caldwell Community College, although she claims fourth grade as her favorite spot to fall. She has been instrumental in preserving local North Carolina stories through oral history projects that have resulted in several narrative nonfiction books set in western North Carolina. Her 2013 children's picture book, *When Christmas Feels Like Home*, is based on her personal experiences of adapting to a new culture during a student exchange program to Lima, Peru. In addition to newspaper and e-magazine articles, she has published in *Highlights for Children*.

www.gretchengriffith.com

Made in the USA
Lexington, KY
22 June 2018